Flesh of Evolution

Our Heritage and Its Effect on Christianity

Collin Smith

ISBN: 0692648232
ISBN-13: 978-0692648230 (Smith)

DEDICATION

To my mother, the first person to believe in me.

FLESH OF EVOLUTION

CONTENTS

FLESH OF EVOLUTION

ACKNOWLEDGMENTS

To those who keep my mind on track, you know who you are, and your guidance is much appreciated.

Cover art courtesy of Kaitlin Kalan.

FLESH OF EVOLUTION

PREFACE

A long period of struggle with creation and evolution preceded this writing. I started off long ago as a creationist, but once I started to look into the matters of creation science, I quickly switched to a type of day-age creationism. There I stayed for some time, building my belief by reading any number of well-written books on the evidence of God in creation, especially those from the field of intelligent design. My learning came quite a ways, and I felt I had a strong position, until I began reading the evolutionary literature. Stubborn as ever, I set out to prove it wrong, thinking that there must be holes in the armor somewhere. Indeed, there are holes in the armor of evolution, but they are fairly small and usually based on hearsay. The further I dug, the more it began to seem like the world has evolved, and I hated it. I knew that evolution didn't necessarily have stakes in the question of God's existence, but it seemed incomprehensible why God would use evolution when it is a horribly imperfect and nasty process. After a while, I settled upon the fact that even if evolution is false, I was not personally going to be able to disprove it, thus removing myself from taking a side on the issue.

And yet, the idea that evolution might be true began to grow on me, challenging my mind to think in new ways. Most notable is the heritage of evolution in the human race. God creating the animal kingdom through evolution seemed strange, but God forming His beloved humans through evolution felt as though it was bordering on heresy. The difficulties of reconciling human evolution with traditional Christian theology pestered my mind, producing no clear answers. With this whirlwind of thoughts came the notion that perhaps evolution is irrelevant. If evolution could potentially be reconciled with Christian theology, then asking whether evolution is true or not is the wrong question. I needed to first and foremost ensure that evolution is entirely compatible with the Christian faith, for all the literature had been approaching this issue from the wrong angle. No one had fleshed out the connections between evolution and Christianity that had begun to fascinate me, and so this work sprang forth. It is very much a new field of thought with uncharted waters, but I could not ignore the way I was being drawn to it.

It is not my intention to convince anyone that evolution is true. It is not my intention to convince anyone that evolution is false. This work focuses on what is much more important: understanding that evolution does nothing to lessen the principles of the Christian faith, but may actually enhance them in some cases. Personally, I do think evolution is true and it was necessary to take such a stance to write this work, but I hold nothing against those who believe creationism. My goal is purely to ensure that people do not reject evolution because they think it is dangerous for the faith. It would be a shame for the Christian Church to lose its impact on society simply because no one took the time to understand how an evolutionary viewpoint could actually threaten their beliefs, if at all, or perhaps even strengthen them.

That's not to say accepting evolution will be easy once it is no longer a threat to a person's faith, and this work certainly reflects that. It is thought provoking and discusses deep questions, the answers to which may be difficult to accept, so it is best read slowly and carefully. It does not lend itself to a clear subdivision, but the sections build upon one another as new ideas and the applications of old ideas are introduced. The foundational reasons for investigating evolution and the resistance against such endeavors first need to be established, and then the implications of evolution can be investigated. Understanding our evolutionary bodies shines an interesting new light on Christianity that subtly shifts the understanding of the Christian message. If we think of the biblical story of redemption as a puzzle, most of it has been firmly established. Christ is at the center of this puzzle's picture, with fundamental doctrines surrounding him. Evolution does not change this picture, as it shouldn't. But evolution also isn't absent from the puzzle. It adds a large number of pieces to the fringes. These supplemental pieces, while not altering the interior pieces, do significantly shift the perception of the puzzle as a whole. An understanding of evolution has the potential to enlighten the viewpoint of Christianity, but it must not nullify the fundamental principles.

I am not a theologian, so although the fundamental principles of Christianity are dealt with in this work, they may not be covered in the most scholarly and complete manner. I leave it to the experts to provide firm ground for Christian doctrines. My goal is to take what has been established and relate it to the findings of evolution. It does not take much research to realize that there is friction between Christian doctrine and evolutionary theory, and as a scientifically minded person still grounded in Christianity I intend to solve these problems. I am the first to admit that I am not qualified to be an authority on either evolution or theology. Still, I am attempting to do what few have thought of: to build strong Christian belief from a foundation of evolution.

A few clarifications about terms need to be made at this point. Any time I use the term *spirit*, I am referring to the human spirit. The Holy Spirit, on the other hand, is always specified directly. Further, *soul* and *spirit* are used interchangeably to mean the human essence which is immaterial, with greater use given to the latter term. Finally, the terms *body*, *flesh*, and *animal* are commonly used to signify the same thing: physical human body. However, *body* is a neutral term used to represent an innocent human body, whereas *flesh* and *animal* are both used to describe a human body that is in the grips of sin, especially with respect to the former.

This work is written primarily for Christians, and as such, any plural personal pronoun refers to the people of the Christian Church. But the ideas of this work are also very important for those outside of Christianity who are struggling to understand how they can support evolution and still follow Christ. It is my hope that this work will bring down the walls that separate evolution and Christianity. And more importantly, it is my hope that this work will bring down the walls that separate evolutionary Christians from creationist Christians. We are called to be one Body.

OF CHIMP OR GOD?

People like to know their heritage. Especially in the melting pot that is the United States, ancestry has become a very popular subject. For whatever reason, we like to know what nationality of people, or combination of nationalities, has produced us. As a displaced orphan wants to know his birthplace, we want to know the circumstances of our ancestral origins. There is a belief that it can help our sense of identity, although it hardly affects daily life in a significant way. It is a human inclination to understand our past in order to grasp who we are today; no other animal has such a desire. For, ultimately, humans are introspective beings who yearn for identity, and ancestry can have a significant role in that process.

Even though it involves the distant past, any investigation of human ancestry should really focus on the first humans. Questions of nationalistic ancestry are insignificant compared to the inquiry of human origins. One compares slightly different races of humans (which have remarkable genetic similarity). The other compares humans to the completely distinct entity that was the source of their origins. As most people are aware, there are two answers to this inquiry when considering the physical human existence. Either we evolved from hominids or were made by the hands of God from the dust of the ground. Even discounting any spiritual aspect of humans, this question is of monumental importance: either we sprung forth from the "factory" of nature or were uniquely forged in God's furnace and dropped among nature.

In Christian circles, the latter option is predominant, and the former is

4

dispelled as demeaning to humankind. If God proclaimed us unique, there's no way we could be the same as the rest of nature. What results is a sort of Buzz Lightyear (referring to a character in the film *Toy Story*) complex. In this view, humans were created in some far-off land and brought to this world unique. We become aloof and unable to identify with nature because we believe our origins are wholly above and beyond this world. Without casting the typical judgement on such a view, this is the mind-set of many Christians. It is not necessarily good or bad. Perhaps we are entirely justified in being aloof from the rest of nature. This mind-set is simply the perception many Christians develop toward the world when a fundamental belief is that we were created exclusively by the hands of God.

But what if we come to realize that we are not unlike the rest of the toys? What if we are a product of nature and deeply connected to this world? In this case, our heritage changes significantly. Actually, our heritage becomes remarkably longer. The human genetic fingerprint was brought to us from the rest of nature through evolution. We are genetically connected to every other organism in the world, and therefore, our heritage is thoroughly embedded in this world. We cannot simply stand aloof. As abstract as it may sound, we are a part of nature and nature is a part of us.

Imagine being in close, friendly proximity to a chimpanzee. You recline peacefully and it mills about playfully around you. If we evolved from nature, that chimp is nothing less than your distant relative. Many Christians squirm at this idea, believing it is both repulsive and condescending toward humans. Unfortunately, there is no simply antidote for this; there is nothing that can be said which will make heritage with chimps more appetizing. At the same time, the idea should not be avoided. We need to sit with this idea and comes to terms with it. If the plausibility of evolution is the problem personally, there are plenty of works by biologists that are sufficiently explanatory, although displaying evidence is not the intent of this work. Even if evolution is untrue, we are in no place to enter a discussion of its implications if we find even the most basic concept of it repulsive. Coming to terms with the possibility of descending from the rest of nature is the first step toward investigating the Christian approach to evolution. Then, the more complex consequences of evolving from nature can be explored. Modifications can be made such that the foundation of Christianity is not damaged and our true position among nature can be understood. But if we cannot first stomach evolution, there is no way we will digest it in a meaningful way.

FOLLOWING GOD IN EVOLUTION

Where is God in the conflict between evolution and creationism? On the other hand, where is the work of Satan? With the division it creates in Christianity, the simple view would be to suppose that one side must be right and the other wrong, therefore dictating which side God is on. However, perhaps holding correct beliefs is not necessary to abide by the will of God, and false beliefs are not necessarily the result of Satan's direct influence. One could be incorrect in the details of his or her beliefs and still live a life truly dedicated to God. Certainly, the proposal that truth is not always a quality of following God is a questionable supposition. But maybe when it comes to following God there is a difference between having wisdom and possessing specific truths.

Examining Christian eschatology is a good example of this idea. There is a substantial variety of opinions about how and when the end times will arrive. Yet, few people would maintain that having the correct eschatology is a necessity of salvation. Lacking this specific truth does not nullify the possession of wisdom in the pursuit of God. Even so, a belief about the end times can also be obviously problematic, such as the belief that evil will not be conquered. In this case, not only is truth absent, but wisdom to follow God is forfeited because the belief contradicts the foundations of God's word. So, if evolution is purely a matter of correct knowledge and does not violate the principles of God's word (a questionable supposition at the present time), then asking which side God is on might be the wrong question. Undoubtedly, only one explanation can be correct (either

7

evolution is true or it isn't) and God must know which one is real truth, but following God may not depend on this belief if the ability to live wisely for God can be found by those on either side.

Thus, the lines become much more blurred than those we'd like to draw. Essentially, truly following God is possible for those on either side of the spectrum, because living wisely can theoretically be approached from the perspective of evolution or creation. It is similar to the denominations of Christianity. There are not separate groupings of those who are saved and those who are not saved based purely on their denomination, for the lines are not only much more complicated than that, but they are also invisible to the non-divine eye. There is no reason to believe it cannot be the same situation for the creation and evolution dichotomy. The questions of our origins have always fascinated us, but that does not exclude the possibility that they are inconsequential to having a relationship with God. Surely, they are less essentially connected to our relationship with God than church practices, and we have little difficulty admitting that our engagement with these practices, or lack thereof, has no direct bearing on our salvation.

At the same time, there is an important distinction to be made. Although members of all Christ-centered denominations have the capacity to attain salvation, certain systems of belief make it more difficult to follow God than others. In this case, the particular truths that are held do not necessarily nullify any possibility of attaining a relationship with God, but can certainly put unseen barriers in the process. To make matters more complicated, the correctness of these truths might be distinct from their effect on people's journey to God. Likewise, it is quite possible that there is a similar situation between creation and evolution. Although evolution may appear to be more reasonable based on evidence, it is at this point not a sufficient way for someone to wisely follow God because of the unseen barriers it creates.

As it stands, the connections between evolution and Christian theology have not been fleshed out to the extent that a genuine relationship with God can be confidently formed based on true theology and an evolutionary framework. People have certainly looked at evolution and concluded that it is not outside the realm of possibility in the Christian faith, but the doctrine of evolution still poses serious threats for anyone who attempts to correctly understand God.

There are simply too many questions that have never been asked nor answered:

Why did God use evolution? How does living in an evolutionary world change our perceptions of God? Are we the same as every other animal? Why are animalistic behaviors considered sinful when a human does them, if we are simply following in the process through which God made us? Why was Jesus' healing an apparent counterforce against the normal workings of nature? How were thousands of years of isolated human tribes saved? Why does it seem we are struggling with the flesh? How are we to treat an imperfect creation made through the contemptable process of evolution?

Life is a constant adaptation and reconnecting of society's circumstances with the perfection of God while being ever cautious to leave the trueness of God undistorted. And although evolution is not society's biggest issue right now, it is one of the largest "gorillas in the room" to be glossed over by the church.

The end goal also brings us more questions. For example, is the battle between evolution and creation over once evolution can be reconciled with theology? Certainly, it ceases to take on the stakes of a battle, but the debate over truth will never and should never stop. Again, consider the Christian denominations. Even though there are distinctions among them, and members will admit that the others are not excluded from salvation, they do not cease to use reason and logic to argue over who holds the correct truth. Arguing can have nasty downsides, but the pursuit of truth overall is nevertheless a worthwhile goal. The fact that these truths in particular are not crucial to salvation should not halt the progress toward attaining these truths. Likewise, even if Christian evolutionists and Christian creationists can have equal access to salvation, the dispute regarding the truth of creation and evolution should not cease. The pursuit of truth should always be cultivated; now there is freedom to journey wherever reason and evidence may take this pursuit, because it does not bear the weight of the Christian faith on one side or the other.

There is also the difficult question of God's intentions. Why would God allow so many people to be convinced of evolution if it isn't true? On the flip side, why would God have allowed people down the path of deistic creationism if it was ultimately to be proven false? In other words, what are God's intentions with giving us the dichotomy of evolution and creationism? As difficult of a question as it is to answer, the opposing side is much clearer. From the perspective of Satan, the goal is obviously to drive Christians apart, with the creation-versus-evolution issue being the wedge. If this issue is built up to be very important in our minds, it will only further Satan's goals by creating artificial divisions in the Christian faith that do not need to be there.

With this in mind, God's intentions become clearer. When presented with an issue that threatens to drive us apart, it may very well be a challenge to hold together in the face of diversity as we focus on what is really central (1 Cor 12:12-13). The beginning of the church witnessed such a dichotomy when Christian Jews and Christian Gentiles created distinctions between their respective spheres of tradition. And yet, once each viewpoint was understood in relation to the pillars of Christ's message, it became clear that the divisions were frivolous. It could very well be the same situation with creation and evolution. Once evolution is established as a viewpoint that doesn't damage the Gospel message, the opinions of those partaking in the origins debate can be set aside when considering the unity of the Christian Church.

This gives way to an important application. Often times in the creation-evolution debates, creationists act as if the weight of Christianity is on their side. The thought goes that if individuals truly pursue God and seek His guidance, He will reveal to them that creationism is true. This is not only misguided but also highly dangerous. It is misguided because not even Genesis 1 is that close-minded. To say that Genesis allows exclusively for a creationist's viewpoint is to stretch well beyond what can be supported by the text. Interpreting as metaphorical what is not only quite poetic but also a miniscule portion of the entire Scriptures is nowhere near a blatant disregard for the authority of Scripture. Is God really going to uniquely reveal to someone the specifics of a poem in His Scriptures when we are all struggling to fathom His love and follow in the life of Christ? It is unfair to say that those who maintain a symbolic interpretation of Genesis 1 are against Christianity and will necessarily be weeded out by God when there are much more critical principles that must be considered.

But more importantly, this viewpoint is very dangerous. In essence, it creates limited access to passage through the gates that lead to the Kingdom of God. The claim that a true pursuit of God requires adherence to creationism forces people into an artificial mold that is unnecessary. The early church had the same problem when Jewish Christians required Gentile Christians to adopt Jewish customs. It stifled the ability of people to come to Christ, and God quickly put an end to it because of the serious harm it could bring to the church. Whether someone is a Jew or Gentile, creationist or evolutionist, becomes irrelevant at the foot of the Cross. The same accusation of believing they are favored by God could be leveled at evolutionary Christians, but they are a minority at the present time and in no place to be tempted by such pride. And yet, it is important, in the end, to realize that the equality of creation and evolution as a route to God supposes that an evolutionary foundation can be reconciled with Christian theology, which is the subject to be dealt with hence forth.

GOD'S NECESSARY ACTS

Undoubtedly, evolution has the ability to inflict destructive consequences on the pillars of the Christian faith. Most notably, it threatens to take away the possibility that there could be purpose and value in human life. If we are all nothing more than highly developed hominids (bipedal apes physically like humans), everything breaks down. From the perspective of evolution, by definition, the only value you can assign to another person is based on the degree to which that person could potentially advance your genetic heritage. Evolution will not cause an organism, in general, to value something that cannot benefit the individual's reproduction.

At first glance, it seems as though evolution can be disproven immediately, because we are constantly in relationships with people who do nothing to advance our genes. However, the legacy of an ancestral environment is much more subtle than that. Relationships and care for other people would have evolved among a group of hominids in a much harsher situation than we know today. By applying the principles of reciprocal altruism (I scratch your back, and you scratch mine) in such a situation it becomes clear that a gift to a friend in need will have more value to the friend than it does to you. This can still be seen today, as a meal for a homeless man has significantly more value to him than it does to someone with a pantry of food.

What would result in the original environment is a debt to the giver when the tables are switched. The receiver of the gift is socially required to return above and beyond the original value of the gift when a need arises for the original giver. So in a situation where mortality rates are high, having connections could mean the difference between life and death. By way of analogy, it is as if hominids in an ancestral setting could buy insurance. The difference is that payments came from both specific alliances and the community at large that had witnessed the individual's previous investment in the community.

From an evolutionary perspective, the apparent advantage of people surrounded by support would continue to surface in modern times, even though we live in a much more forgiving environment. Our constant desire for relationships and our valuing of others who do not confer reproductive advantages are not necessarily snags for evolution, because our pre-human ancestors could have had very good reason to network with other individuals. Creating an interdependent community, although not directly benefiting the individual, could have been crucial when resources became scarce and death came quickly to those who carved their own path.

However, there is a more substantial dissonance between the principles of evolution and the workings of human life. This is best illustrated by the defeat of Nazi Germany. To begin, it can be affirmed that the actions of Nazi Germany are within the principles of natural selection. Clan mentality, which strives to eliminate outsiders (and their genes), is completely understandable from this perspective. In an ancestral environment, nationalistic or regional passions would surely have been cultivated, and we can even see the equivalent today in the warfare between tribes of chimps. The clan of humans most zealously devoted to one another would clearly have an advantage over those who lacked a desire for universal identity.

The efforts of the Allied forces to subdue Nazi Germany are also within evolutionary reason. When a neighboring clan begins to display signs of aggression, the natural tendency is to defend one's own group. At the same time, in defeating the Nazis, the Allied forces went a step further than can be supported by evolutionary theory. It was in affirming that the Nazis were undoubtedly violating the intrinsic value of humans through the genocide of Jews that the allies went beyond what can be justified by the principles of natural selection. We can see this affirmation of universal human value in our daily lives too, although not with the clear parallel to an undoubtedly frequent scenario for pre-humans. As central as it is to human existence, we must confront the fact that evolution, by definition, knows of no intrinsic value within humans.

Indeed, it could be supposed that the belief in universal human value is a residual feeling based on a general selection that favored those who viewed other people as possessing some potential importance in their lives. But this is problematic, for although there could have been selection that favored those who viewed people as important, there is also equally strong reasons to believe that an ancestral environment would have favored those who had cultivated a fear of strangers. Even though social connection could have become common, the end goal is still genetic propagation, which could produce a passion for violence that outweighed the inklings for friendship. It is not unreasonable to think that the majority of ancestral tribes were striving for victory and not equality. Thus, although there are reasons to think friendship could have been favored at times, it is certainly not a one-sided coin or even the most dominant of the two forces where survival is the ultimate goal. In this light, the universal value of human life as displayed most powerfully in World War II is without evolutionary merit, because devotion to the friendship of strangers would certainly not have been a dominant trait.

This brings up an interesting topic since evolutionists have conjectured that just because valuing human life is outside the justification of natural selection doesn't mean we shouldn't pursue it. The argument postulates that the human race should decide outside of evolution what is right and wrong. In other words, there should be a distinction between evolutionarily right and humanly right. Yet, there is no reason to believe this is possible in a materialistic world. If everything we are has come from evolution, how can we ever be sure that we are outside of evolution? It has shaped our emotional attachments and desires so much that it would be questionable to suppose any feelings or characteristics in the present time were not similarly created. How can we ever reject evolution when it could have very well selected for the exact thoughts that are rejecting it? Nevertheless, it is still worthwhile to investigate those aspects of human lives that run contrary to evolution, such as the universal value of human life, for it can provide insight to another option: that evolution isn't the whole story.

As it applies to the Christian faith, God using evolution but never setting apart a few hominids (perhaps a pair) and imparting them with an immaterial spirit is entirely unsustainable. The Bible repeatedly affirms that there is universal value in human beings. Jesus rightfully summarizes the Old Testament law as loving God and loving other people as yourself. But loving other people as yourself is completely foreign to evolution, because it would mean assigning a value to them that equals your own. So we are not only given instructions that contradict evolution because of what they say about the value in other people, but the fact that we are theoretically called upon to act according to these commands makes an additional statement. Why tell an animal to stop acting like an animal if it can't possibly happen? God telling us to act outside evolution necessitates that there is something more to humans beyond that possessed by other animals. By looking at the commands integral to the Bible, it becomes clear that there must be something more to humans; they cannot simply be animals controlled by evolution.

If we consider that the essence of a human being consists of both a material body shaped by the forces of this world and an immaterial soul imparted by God, several important consequences result. First, evolution naturally brings with it the idea that humans are just animals governed by biological processes that give the impression of personal being. But the dwelling of a spirit flips this on its head. We can now confidently affirm that we are so much more than animals. If we hold the belief that the soul was added (or continuously added) to the human race, it rescues us from being confined to the reality of delusional animals that only imagine ourselves as having a soul because it is of some competitive gain for the physical body. Personal being is not a mirage; it is a reality.

Additionally, this alters the idea of what it means to be made in the image of God. There is some sense in which all of nature is a reflection of God. The ability to perceive surroundings through sight, sound, touch, and our other senses all parallel God's method of operation, although in a severely limited way. So, in-as-much as they possess these commonalities of nature, our bodies are a reflection of God. But the reasoning stops there. Our bodies do not make us unique among creation. The physical appearance of the human body has nothing to do with possessing the image of God. Having an advanced nervous system that can reason in rudimentary ways and take in information from the surroundings likely has a connection to God, but even chimps possess these abilities. As much as we'd like to think God has an appearance more like a human than a chimp, there is no reasonable basis for this from the perspective of evolution.

As an important side note, this shift in the image of God has implication for the life of Jesus. If our bodies are not the image of God, then Christ was not being born into something he was already familiar with. Rather, he was submitting himself to the wretched body of an animal. There is a general idea that the sinless divine combined with a body originally created by God formed an image that very much resembled God. Yet, under the view of evolution, Jesus was truly humbling himself to the level of dirt. Apart from a well-developed nervous system to support a conscience soul with complex senses, he might as well have come to the body of a worm. This is a crucial point. There is nothing about our physical bodies and the arrangements of molecules within them that makes us any better than the lowest of creatures. He did not simply come to a fallen human race, but to the sufferable body of an animal. Adopting a human body was submitting to a position lower than we could possibly imagine, for the bodies we adore are no better than those of the most despicable animals. An animal is nothing in relation to God, even if that animal has a human body.

If the image of God is void in our physical appearance, then where is it located? The simple answer would be to suppose that it resides solely in the spirit, but this is inaccurate. The entire human being is a reflection of God, and although the body is not significant on its own, it is nonetheless foundational to the larger picture. This brings up an important point, for any consideration of the duality of humans in which the body existed before the spirit is bound to result in a degrading stance toward the body. The human spirit contains everything that pertains to being a human, and it just happens to occupy a body. Yet, this does not do justice to God's creation of humans and the accompanying decrees about the state of humanity. The human spirit without a human body is not a human, and the human body without the human spirit is not a human. Only when the body and spirit are combined does a true human exist. It is like combining two colors to produce a third color. Yes, the properties of the initial colors influence the final color, but green cannot be separated into blue and yellow while still being considered green. And it is the final product that is in the image of God. The totality of the human is in the image of God, and if the body of a human is removed from the spirit, a significant portion of this image is lost.

The image of God is not captured in the snapshot of a human. We are not statues that resemble God in the formulas of our composition; rather, the image of God is an active quality that plays out as we display life. When we build loving relationships, nurture strong communities, and become bonded to one another, we are displaying the image of God as a relational being. When we discover a deeper understanding of the natural world and design new ways of expressing the complexities of humanity, we are displaying the image of God as a creative being. And when we responsibly rule over nature, establish human societies, and preserve God's creation, we are displaying the image of God as a sovereign being. Our creation as a reflection of God is seen through the activity of human life as it was meant to be, not in the snapshot of a human that somehow evokes divine qualities.

At the same time, an active image of God still requires a fundamental change in constitution when considering evolution. As will be seen later in our discussion, a life that mirrors the character of God is unattainable by an animal. It cannot love unconditionally, or think and create symbolically, or be a steward above the rest of nature. For humans to truly be made in the image of God, they needed to be more than an animal, which is where the immaterial spirit becomes important. Although the spirit is not the entirety of our divine image, it is the cornerstone that makes it possible. By living as embodied creatures in which the spirit is in authority over the body, we are able to live as more than animals and possess a greater image of God among creation. The alteration in our constitution in which the spirit was given embodied dominion of the flesh is crucial to being able to represent God from within the confines of nature. Perhaps even animals have spirits, although from observation this spirit must not have dominion over the body, because animals always act within the confines of materialistic nature. What's important is that in humans the immaterial spirit was given dominion over the body, and the image of God was able to be on display through our lives.

INTERROGATING THE CREATOR

There are few questions more difficult to consider than why God would use evolution. Although considering God's intentions in using evolution is entirely legitimate, the assumptions that undoubtedly accompany this question are perhaps the larger problem. The vast majority of times that we are troubled at the prospect of God in evolution, what we are actually resisting is a decrease in the power of God. After all, it would be infinitely more divine to create something from nothing in a miraculous display of power rather than reshape what is already existing, albeit in a messy way. Clearly, God still possesses this power, but its absence in creation doesn't fit with human preconceptions. His decision to not use a power we know is present challenges us to reconcile our minds with the fact that someone who is all-powerful may choose to not use that power. Not only does human nature tell us that power should always be utilized, but it is our tendency to believe God should reflect this ideology. God the Son came without transcendent displays of divine power, and no one was able to understand how such a feeble king could be God (Lk 4:22). That's not to say that God's power is not working through natural processes such as evolution, but simply that it is not the obvious power we expect from God.

Why are we insistent upon affirming that God divinely created the beautiful landscapes of nature? We don't hesitant to proclaim that the same God who formed us also shaped with His hands the bursting of color in sunsets, rising strength of mountains, or deep mystery of a forest. A simplistic association between God and power is partly responsible, but this explanation is far from complete. Times of uncertainty (as seem to never end) inevitably lead to a zeal for certainty. So then, if we cannot witness God's power directly in the manifestations of nature all around us, who is to say that He really has power over the day-to-day miseries of our lives? Believing His power is evident in the remarkable aspects of nature builds what we think is a suitable foundation for His authoritative role in our lives, and this providence is not convincing when we witness an evolved world. Obviously, this logic was proved preposterous once and for all after what happened on Resurrection Sunday, but that does nothing to lessen its repeated appearance in human thought.

The radical effect this has on our idea of God is crucial. It is as if we need to abandon the perception that we are living in a house built directly by the hands of our Father. We have become lulled into the comfort of seeing the fingerprints of God in such natural beauties as the rock layers of the Grand Canyon or the complexity of a cell. Even when trials came, we could be assured of the coziness and security of a home built by the hands of our loving Father, because we thought the signs were all over the walls. But now, with this alternate understanding, it is as if God hired independent contractors to do the job, removing our direct connection to Him in place of a middle man. The world becomes much more cold and frightening when we can no longer witness the hands of God in this house. We are forced into the perception of an alien living in foreign soil where he has no business being. So we refuse to release the concept of God's intervention in nature not only because it gives Him power, but more importantly because that power manifested through the creation of our home provides the security a human soul yearns for.

Or can we see God in nature? Surely, we cannot witness the fingerprint of God in the way we may want to. In previous times we may have gazed upon the feathers of a peacock and marveled at the hand of God, but it is now clear that this is only an illusion. Sexual selection made those intricately designed feathers, and there is little question about this from a scientific standpoint. And yet, this doesn't seem to bother many Christians, and there is a reasonable, albeit suppressive, explanation for this perspective. Christians will at one time admit that God did not directly make the feathers of a peacock if and only if they can maintain the belief that there is some dividing line between where evolution stops and God's hand begins. He may not have made the peacock specifically, but He certainly created different classes of birds as a whole. In other words, the notion that God is still the creator is suppressed within the hope that there was some point in the ancient past when God's hand was independently decreeing the beauty of nature that natural selection would then maintain through changing environments.

But is it really logical to draw this arbitrary line? Even if we could draw an imaginary line between those species of common ancestor and those that are distinct, is it justifiable to suddenly decree that the forces of selection that we admit are present within these individual groups suddenly became ineffective? There appear to be distinct classes of animals today, but with over 98 percent of all species ever to live on Earth extinct, who is to say that the environment wasn't much more fluid in the past?

Hiding the role of God in nature within some marvelous acts in the distant past seems like a slippery slope. One day we could be declaring these imaginary distinctions, and years later they could be flushed down the drain of disproven hypothesizes, perhaps with the rest of the Christian faith. Indeed, the church in the time of Galileo experienced such a crucial adaptation in its beliefs. Church leaders passionately believed that the earth was the center of the universe, as supposedly taught by the Bible. But for all the stock that was put in this issue with regard to the authority of God, it was resolved without destruction to the Christian faith. Likewise, the hope of God's divine action in the recesses of the past to drive out materialistic explanations in nature needs to be released if the Christian faith is to be built on solid ground. This is not a situation, as many would like to believe, when science is able to abuse faith. It is an examination of the central pillars of the faith and coming to an understanding of what can be released for the benefit of faith as a whole.

Consider God as a cartoon magician. With divine ingenuity, He waves His magical wand, a little pixie dust flies, and an animal appears, right? This is how divine action works in the modern mind. Something appears out of nothing and almost always very quickly. But what if God doesn't work that way? Clearly, God could make something fully formed out of nothing if He so desired, but perhaps He simply chooses not to. In essence, the question of whether God can be seen in evolution comes down to challenging the idea of what it means for God to "move His magical wand." Perhaps, instead of an animal appearing out of nothing, there is a mutation within the genome of a certain animal, and for thousands of years God's hand is continuing to move as that gene becomes propagated within a population isolated from its ancestors. Although it may be unsatisfying to witness God only through the work of secondary forces, presuming that God's action needs to appear as we think it should is certainly a simplistic view of God constrained by the limitations of human understanding. In addition, this does not rule out the possibility of miracles beyond physical explanation, but simply expands the idea of what it means to witness God's hand at work.

Although it may seem far-fetched, isn't this how we view God in our own lives? A Christian will not hesitate to affirm that God was at work in a particular situation resolving itself, even though there could be physical causes to explain why something happened. Furthermore, we find it much more suitable to see God in physical processes at large. The continents were once in very different places than they are now and have moved to their current positions due to plate tectonics, but a Christian may have no problem recognizing that God could have been at work even though there are testable explanations. Stars and planets form out of a process involving interatomic forces, particularly gravity, among matter on a large scale, and yet God's hand is seen there too.

Perhaps it is because of the distance from our personal lives. While not being able to affirm God's fingerprint in the planets or geological processes has little effect on the coziness of our daily lives, admitting that the squirrel that just ran past was shaped through millions of years of biological processes hits much too close to home. Or maybe it is simply the pedestal we have built life up to be. Apart from every other physical process in the world, life has always been unique, even to the point of hypothesizing a "vital force" within it. Conceding that life was shaped through material processes just like everything else certainly appears to take a large bite out of what was once reserved for the divine.

And yet, life is still special. Just because it was made by evolution doesn't imply it would have happened without God. This is a crucial distinction between materialistic evolution and a Christian perspective on evolution. Only through a belief in God can someone claim that evolution would not have happened without God, because an evolutionary world fails to display divine handiwork in most cases. It takes faith to know that someone was present when the scene has no conclusive signs of that person's fingerprints. In fact, God holds ALL of the world up through physical processes in a way we will never understand (Col 1:17), and it takes faith to witness Him when this house does not show the marks of His hand. To say that the action of God must look radically different than the day-to-day processes of nature is to discount the deep connection God has with His creation. He is working through nature just as much now as He has been for billions of years, which includes the processes of evolution.

Thus, there is a sharp distinction in our perceptions. We cannot look at the sunset and proclaim that God painted its beauty with His divine power, but at the same time He is moving in that sunset just as He is moving in everything around us. There are real molecular and optical reasons for a sunset, but faith in God adds the crucial belief that God is orchestrating it all from behind the curtain of our intellect. Life certainly becomes colder when God's fingerprints are absent from nature. All beauty is no longer bursting with the color of God, but is merely a shadow of Him. Life is transformed into a constant struggle to discover God among the shades of an uncomforting world.

This results in a dilemma, for if Genesis 1 is to be taken metaphorically through a different view of God's handiwork, who is to say that Genesis 2 should not also be revisited? Surely, a metaphorical interpretation in Genesis 1 does not nullify the diverse truths of Scripture, but it still has an effect on the interpretation of Genesis 2. In short, an evolutionary view changes the creation of mankind but also does not change it. On the one hand, it gives new meaning to "the dust of the ground" (Gen 2:7). From the traditional viewpoint, God is seen as literally taking mud and shaping it into humans. Although it is within His power to instantaneously change the simple organic molecules of dirt into those required for life, it is perhaps equally likely that He used preexisting hominids. Hominids shaped by evolution truly would be made from dust; it simply would have been over the course of millions of years. In that sense, evolution shifts the perspective of God's preexisting "building materials."

But at the same time, the influence of evolution needs to be rejected on one crucial point. God must have imparted a spirit among these hominids. There is no clear physical evidence for this, but rather it is a matter of looking at the truths of the Bible and realizing what cannot be compromised. The value of human life as sustained throughout Scripture can only be reconciled with an evolutionary foundation if God imparted a spirit to humans (as discussed in 'God's Necessary Acts"). While affirming that nature was made through evolution is uncomfortable, it does not destroy the pillars of the Christian faith. A lack of intrinsic human value completely abolishes the meaning of what Jesus did at the cross, for it was the ultimate declaration of universal human value, which cannot be maintained by materialistic evolution.

In essence, connections between evolution and theology are not a one-way street. Theology can have something to say too. With that in mind, how can the theory that God created each type of species (especially the hominids) be tested with the God we know from the Bible? This is a common day-age creationist interpretation that reconciles God's intervention with the deep time of geology, and it is important to consider its relation to the God of the Bible. Upon contemplation, there is a clear contradiction. If, for ages upon ages, God was exercising His divine power through the incredible acts of species formation, He must have suddenly had a change of heart by taking a less active role once humans were created. Think about it. If humans were made forty to one hundred thousand years ago with civilizations sustaining generation upon generation, imagine the sheer amount of human souls that not only struggled to survive more than much of modern civilization but also lived without ever witnessing God. That's not to say He never did anything and was not constantly moving in natural processes, but the most obvious witness to God's intervention must have come in the form of the history of the Israelite nation. Yet, within this history, His action is not only sparse, but is nothing compared to the divine creation of an animal.

So what does human history tell us about God? Clearly, He is an unseen God (Jn 1:18). Direct and awe-inspiring divine action comes only very rarely. So why would it be reasonable to think that God was a much more active participant in the ancient past? Believing that God was moving powerfully in the creation of the animal and plant kingdoms over billions of years produces a dichotomy to the God witnessed in history. God is notoriously silent, or at least partially obstructed. A display of unquestionable divine power is witnessed only very rarely.

This shifts all of the attention to Jesus. This was a God unseen for billions of years becoming something everyone could witness. We cannot look at the sunset and see God directly, and although this is depressing, it need not stop there. The absence of God in the beauty of this house around us should become entirely irrelevant when God Himself comes and knocks on the door. True, evolution makes this world cold and alien, but that should only make us cling tighter to the one who showed us our true citizenship. Furthermore, a silent perspective on the actions of God in nature since the beginning of time adds greater weight to Jesus's actions as a man. His humility cannot be overstated. A boxer who has been itching for billions of years to enter the ring should come with a bang, not with twelve fickle companions and a death sentence.

GENETIC SELFISHNESS

Behind all of nature there are genes, short strands of DNA or RNA that encode for the information necessary to sustain an organism and allow it to reproduce. Most people understand this, and some even look upon this aspect of nature with a personal sense of wonder. But what many people don't understand is the driving force that permeates every single organism. The goal of every strand of genetic information ever synthesized is to create more copies of itself by any means necessary, even if that means killing off the surrounding organisms. All of nature is selfish at the level of the individual, even if it doesn't appear that way. To the human eye, there appears to be a lot of cooperation and peaceful relations, but this is simply a facade. Although members of a species (or different species) may be mutually helpful to one another's survival, this is only the complex network unfolded by evolution in which individuals exhibit care for others purely because it will be a benefit to themselves. When many genetically identical cells combine to form the larger organisms we are all familiar with, the interactions between these organisms can become intricate. But make no mistake: That organism is only alive to find some clever way to reproduce more of itself.

Many of the problems that arise in the maintenance of the human body stem from the exact same source of genetic selfishness. Consider the common flu. A virus is made up of a stand of genetic information surrounded by an encasement of proteins. This genetic information only contains what is necessary for reproducing itself and synthesizing the necessary structural proteins. The virus isn't even alive. It must inject its genetic information into a living cell and force the cell to reproduce the virus. Then, the colony of newly made viruses burst out of the now dead cell (hence the flu symptoms) with only one purpose: to make more copies of its simple genetic sequence. Humans get the flu, quite simply, because a short genetic sequence wants to replicate itself at our expense. What happens if the virus is unabated in these efforts? All human life dies and the virus can no longer replicate (assuming it can't transfer to a new species). It doesn't care. Its goal, along with the goal of every other set of genes, is complete genetic domination. Some organisms are more realistic about their short-term methods for this end, and are therefore more cooperative, but they all have unrelenting selfishness.

This is the basis for evolution. Complete selfish desire at the individual level creates competition that drives progress forward. If every organism was content with its own little space of nature, there would be no competition. But every organism wants to reproduce itself as much as possible, so someone's bound to draw the short straw. Those with the greatest level of fitness due to a unique set of genes are able to have the greatest presence in the subsequent generations, creating a directionality to change in which the "weaker" qualities become more and more nonexistent. In reality, the qualities of fitness may have little to do with an organism's ability to survive (e.g., peacock feathers), but competition still creates a directionality in which certain members of a species have a larger genetic heritage than others. Combine this with limited resources, interspecies competition, and genetic mutation, and Mother Nature has a potent cocktail on her hands.

With genetic selfishness being so central to evolution, it is essential to consider it in relation to Christian doctrine. But first, it must simply be considered in relation to the human race. And this is most easily done through an aspect of evolution that has widely dominated human society: sexual reproduction. The reasons for sexual reproduction having arisen from asexual reproduction are complicated, but what is hardly complicated is the driving force behind sex. Once sexual reproduction was established, it is no surprise why it became dominant in all affected species. A greater amount of sex means greater genetic heritage for the individual organism. In other words, the entire goal of evolution is met through sex; thus, it grabbed onto this action and associated it with, most notably, intense pleasure. But it also defined many other aspects in an organism's existence based on their influence for sex. Only those individuals with the best displays, or the most stable nests, or the most resources are able to have sex. And in many cases, the most dominant individual seizes complete control to the rights for sex within a boundary. Among ape communities, it is not uncommon for physical abuse to ensue after a subordinate is found copulating with a female in the jurisdiction of the dominant male.

With the idea of genetic selfishness in mind, especially with regard to sex, we can begin to ask some important questions in relation to Christianity. Most notably, what is the significance of Jesus telling men to pluck an eye out if it causes them to look lustfully upon a woman (Mt 5:29)? In the traditional framework, where marriage and intercourse between spouses are establishments of God, there is nothing significant about this statement. The only thing that stands out is the severity of the command. However, within an evolutionary framework everything changes. Male sexual desire is a huge driving force for natural selection, and now Jesus is passionately telling us to turn away from it. This happens with a number of different focal points of passion, such as power, wealth, and revenge, but sexual lust has the most direct connection to evolution. There are indirect reasons why the other desires would be favored in an ancestral environment, but that which is sexual is simply the easiest to recognize. What are we to make of the fact that Jesus' commands against sin are also commands against acting like an animal?

First, it should be affirmed why lusting is wrong. At the heart of it, the reason must be because it is intense desire to the point of idolization of something other than God. Yet, it is interesting that Jesus would give such emphasis to this desire. He also commands on the topics of lust for revenge, power, and money, but He doesn't mention a number of other aspects of lust, most notably that for success (perhaps because it's not always bad). Regardless, a command that includes a plucking out of eyes was clearly taken seriously in this society, and throughout the rest of the New Testament sexual immorality is given special weight, likely as a reflection of Jesus. In Romans, Paul states that those who have forsaken God are given over to sexual desires. Of all the characteristics of the sinful nature, sexual lust is central.

It seems Jesus knows something we don't. Of course, being fully human, he would have understood first hand that sexual desire can be strong and then gave commands based on what he already knew from experience about human life. But, under an evolutionary framework, it can be affirmed that he had some other knowledge up his sleeve. The propagation of genes is the entire goal of evolution. If a desire for sex can be selected for, it will be, because more sex means more genes in the next generation. Sexual lust is the emotion most directly utilized by evolution, and it being ingrained within the programming of our material bodies means Jesus understood He was addressing something that is immensely powerful—hence the forceful commands. To be sure, the other lusts are intricately linked to sexual desire as well. Power, wealth, and even revenge are all ways to get your genes more successfully into the next generation, although they do not seem as such. Sexual lust is simply the pinnacle of all lusts that plague the human flesh, from an evolutionary standpoint.

Thus, a pattern arises. Taking the example of the most powerful desire arising from evolution, one can consider whether it is merely a coincidence that in commanding us to essentially cast away our flesh, Jesus is also saying that God needs to be put in His rightful place. In other words, is the flesh as built by evolution constantly in the business of removing from God that which is rightfully His? This seems entirely possible. Power, wealth, and sex all involve deceptively receiving satisfaction from a mirage that has taken the place of God, and they all have evolutionary underpinnings. Indeed, it is not mere coincidence that everything the flesh tells us to do is exactly the opposite of what we should be doing, for glorifying God should be our ultimate goal, and the propagation of genes does exactly the opposite.

In a strange manner, genes are constantly striving to "glorify" themselves by greater production in the next generation. As previously discussed, genes are entirely selfish and are only concerned with their own propagation. They don't care about the greatness of God. So it should come as no surprise that the process that shaped our material bodies is controlled by the same foundation of self-interest. Jesus is essentially telling us to cast off that which has been shaping the animal kingdom for hundreds of millions of years.

There is an important correlation here. Many of the commands God gives us are exactly the opposite of what evolution wants, for the glorification of genes often entails the glorification of yourself as favored by evolution. Life by the Holy Spirit, as described in Galatians 5, illustrates this parallel direction of evolution and the sinful nature. First on the list (5:19) to describe the sinful nature is sexual immorality, which is to be expected, as previously noted. Apart from witchcraft and idolatry, which are cases in which the spirit is unable to truly seek God (see the section "Side Effects"), the remaining qualities of a life wallowed in sin have justifiable evolutionary reasons. Not only can hatred, discord, jealousy, rage, and envy be ultimately tied to selfishness, but they all have strong evolutionary motivations in an ancestral environment. Those in an ancestral society who looked out for themselves more than anyone else, and therefore reflected these emotions, would have an advantage to propagate more genes in the next generation. Just look at the example of chimpanzees: One doesn't get to be the alpha male by being gentle and forgiving.

Even qualities and behaviors such as drunkenness and participation in orgies have evolutionary underpinnings, for pleasure could have easily been selected for by evolution. The hormones that produce pleasure through sex were likely altered slightly to create a variety of euphoric feelings resulting from different stimuli, thus producing organisms that seek pleasure beyond sex. Gossip seems like an outlier, but it too has subtle evolutionary rewards. In an environment where language was first developed and conditions were very harsh, information was a valuable commodity to be traded like any material, not to mention the higher social stature one gets by bringing someone else down. Thus, the characteristics of the sinful nature are deeply connected to the foundations for evolution not only in the general sense that selfishness produces advantage, but also in a number of strange cases in which the heritage of evolution is difficult to see.

Subtle evolutionary contradictions are seen even within Jesus' command to not do acts of kindness in front of others (Mt 6:1). This command seems to be speaking only to the prideful propensities of humans, but there are actually potential evolutionary reasons why we would want to have our kindness witnessed. In an ancestral environment where kindness for other beings outside one's genetic heritage was first cultivated, reciprocal altruism was a very important concept. As noted earlier, a gift for someone in need has greater value to the receiver than it does to the giver, resulting in a debt to the giver. Obviously, those in today's society do not give to the poor with the intention of the poor someday paying them back. But being viewed in a community as a person who plays his or her part in helping people results in a much greater likelihood that the community will be there to support that individual in a time of need. In contrast, those who steal and therefore exploit society are punished, with fierce punishments being especially common in ancient tribes. So helping people without having anyone else there to witness could potentially contradict the entire reason evolution selected for altruism in certain hominids. There is a deep underlying conviction that how other people perceive us is crucial, especially with regard to kindness, because it could have meant the difference between life and death for our ancestors. This is yet another example of God telling us to reject the desires of our evolutionary heritage.

Isn't the entire message of Jesus' ministry the opposite of what evolution would suggest? The centerpieces He proclaims as the Kingdom of God are humility and love. With regard to humility (Lk 14:11), it is obviously not a genetic advantage to be the lowest of society. Surely, there are situations when it is in the best interest of a subordinate member to submit to a superior, but the universal humility that Jesus preaches would eventually mean death of an organism. Being last when resources are limited could be potentially disastrous for an organism's heritage.

Love, on the other hand, appears to be mildly agreeable with the constructs of evolution. The euphoric feelings associated with it can not only propagate genes, but the desire to be connected with others could also have been selected for (see the section "God's Necessary Acts"). However, Jesus shatters the boundaries of evolutionary precepts by commanding us to love others (including enemies) *as yourself* (Mk 12:31). The only evolutionary value that can be assigned to someone is based on the extent to which that individual can benefit one's genes. So it would be foolishness to serve and benefit others to an extent that equals oneself, because there is no way that individual can benefit one's genes to an equal amount. Unrelenting love is completely foreign to the foundations of evolution. With regard to Jesus's ministry, the entire lifestyle he preaches runs contrary to everything our flesh desires.

In the end, it is crucial to understand the synonymous essence of our sinful nature and desires of the evolution that have been engrained within the flesh. Genetic selection has made animals to be entirely selfish, even in acts of kindness (reciprocal altruism), and living in bodies that have evolved means that our sinful nature has its roots in the desires ingrained by evolution. We have always known that humans are prone to put themselves above God, but evolution would recognize that this is a quality originally present in the physical bodies of humans. And if the flesh is the root of the power behind our sinful nature, then this shifts the perspective of what we are trying to cast off. Jesus' command to pluck out one's eye is a direct command to forsake the principles that built the flesh. Every objective to elevate God above our personal objectives is a matter of rejecting the selfishness that built our bodies.

THE "EVIL" FLESH

All discussion up until this point leads to the conclusion that our flesh is evil. This is not unwarranted, for the consideration of Christianity from the perspective of evolution certainly makes the flesh appear evil. God repeatedly commands people to indirectly forsake the principles of evolution that built their flesh, thus connecting the sinful nature to the desires of evolution. Not only that, but the entire lifestyle the Son of God preached was contrary to evolution. It would certainly appear as though our flesh, and even nature in general, is evil. Yet, we know this is fundamentally problematic. For starters, God's creation is good, as affirmed by His own words. How could it be fundamentally evil? But more importantly, how can our flesh be evil if it is included in the plan for all eternity? God created us with bodies for a reason, and it wasn't so that we could be automatically consumed by evil.

This is one of the fundamental aspects that has been overlooked as Christians have examined the legitimacy of evolution. The foundational principles of evolution compared with the defining acts of sin in the Bible create the very powerful perception that nature must be evil. It is especially problematic for those who suppose complete continuity between evolution and humans as we are today. It has become more prevalent for those in Christian circles who wish to sustain an entirely scientific approach on human origins to assert that God did not intervene in the process of human evolution. The human spirit (or perhaps simply the perception of a spirit) arose naturally from the physical processes, as was always destined to happen.

Not only is continuity in human evolution logically unsustainable (see the section "God's Necessary Acts"), it also has significant problems for the concept of the flesh being considered evil. What God had created was never altered from His original creation when humans came along operating like every other animal, just as God had deemed good. Then, God condemns those very actions in humans that He created in all animals and never altered. Obviously, it is self-contradictory to condemn that which had previously been deemed good. But more importantly, continuity in human evolution removes all culpability from humans. How can we be blamed for being evil if we never had any choice? We're just the next step in evolution, only doing what animals were created to do. At no point did we fall from God's good favor by any choice of our own. Thus, continuity in human evolution is completely unsupported by the truths put forth by the Bible.

There is a much more common position among the few Christians who intend to be at peace with evolution. Many people believe that evolution created human bodies, at which point God imparted His spirit and brought them to a perfect garden where everything unfolded as traditionally supposed. The humans rebelled against God and were condemned to eternal separation from God. There is no fundamental problem with this position, but it still ignores the weight of the sinful connections to the flesh. It could be supposed that the reason there are synonymous aspects between the evolutionary desires of flesh and the sinful nature results naturally from the fact that the whole human being turned against God. The flesh has sinful characteristics simply because the whole human has sinful characteristics. But this is an unsatisfying position, for it fails to give an understanding as to why the sinful qualities of the flesh are defined by evolution. So it does nothing to escape an evil flesh. Many of the ways in which humans display their evil nature are still through an exemplification of the principles of evolution, and why acting within the constructs of evolution is considered sinful lacks an explanation.

Imagine a situation in which a person had been wearing a heavy black jacket for a long period of time and at some point took it off. Then, due to a mishap that was entirely that person's own fault, the clothing underneath became covered with black paint. As part of the consequence, this person was required to put back on the black jacket. At no point in this story is there an explanation as to why the jacket was black and, more importantly, why the color of the jacket matched the color of the paint long before the paint came along. Such is the situation of the perspective of human evolution that tries to return to the traditional idea of the fall. The human spirit experienced death and separation from God (black paint), but also happened to take on a flesh that had already been displaying these signs of separation from God for millennia (black jacket). We know this because God declares as sinful many actions that have been discovered to have been in operating within nature long before humans. We know the jacket is black because God calls it black. Saying that humans display sinful qualities in the flesh simply because the whole human is sinful would be sustainable if these qualities were somehow independent from nature. But that's not what we observe. The sinful qualities displayed by human flesh are identical to those that have been on display in nature from the beginning. How could nature (and our flesh) not be considered evil?

Understanding this snag is crucial. Once it is discovered that many of the actions God defines as sin have evolutionary underpinnings, a simple scenario of human evolution cannot be maintained. God setting apart a couple of advanced hominids formed through evolution is a necessary starting point. But it is unsustainable to suppose a fall identical to that always imagined in which humans spiritually rebelled against God in a manner similar to Satan. It does nothing to explain why these humans would later act like their animal ancestors and be called sinful. A new scenario needs to be imagined if evolution is going to be reconciled with the truths maintained by Christianity.

THE MUTINY

If we must be able to maintain that the flesh is not evil, how do we get to the point where the fundamental principles of the flesh have a defining effect on our sinful nature? Humans frequently display actions indistinguishable from those of animals, and God declares many of these actions sinful. It is not enough to say that the human flesh acts sinful simply because the whole human is sinful. Unless nature is going to be deemed evil, an entirely new framework compared to the traditional story of the fall needs to be realized.

Consider the situation in the Garden of Eden. Advanced hominids were given a spirit so that they could interact personally with God, and for a while they managed to not ravage that relationship. And yet, it is abundantly clear that the first humans desired to unseat God from His throne as a result of the temptation from Satan. The traditional viewpoint maintains that the humans went about unseating God by choosing to give priority to the beings deep down within themselves. They believed their innermost beings were better than God, and submitting to the idolatrous voice within the spirit was the route by which they would overthrow God. With the human spirit taking the reins of human life away from God, condemnation permeated within every crack of the human being. Humans became blackened all the way to the core, and it is every part of them that now must be cleansed of evil.

But is this the most reasonable scenario? Tyrants overthrowing a king will always use what makes them unique to find an edge. Would it be any different for the first humans? To them, God's existence was not material; He did not have a physical body. Why would the first humans choose to use something that was an attribute of God in order to overthrow Him? Looking within themselves for a being that could unseat God meant looking for something immaterial, the spirit. But God existed to them primarily in spirit, and it wouldn't take much analysis to realize His spirit is greater than their own. It would be more reasonable for them to use their physical existence to gain an edge on God because it was something He apparently lacked, and they had considerable dominion over the beautiful physical world around them.

However, the traditional view makes utilization of the physical existence untenable. If God made the human body from scratch, there was nothing within the body that was vying for priority over God. Submitting authority to the body would have been exactly the same as the traditional viewpoint, because it would still be the human spirit listening to its own idolatrous voice. This is where evolution provides a radical new insight. Humans living in evolved bodies would not have had a quiet flesh, for evolution would have been screaming for authority. Their bodies brought something to the table that was not intrinsic to the human spirit: an additional idolatrous voice. The flesh of humans was built upon millions of years of unencumbered reign for the genetically selfish voice of evolution that did everything for the benefit of an organism's genes. Once imparted with a spirit, it was subdued to some extent, but nevertheless hidden within the flesh.

Consider the distinction this makes for desires such as that for food. One could say that because the human body would get hungry with or without evolutionary heritage, the first humans could have given priority to bodies made directly by God through eating the forbidden fruit. But this still wouldn't pin the blame on their bodies. Flesh made directly by God would've had no problem being hungry, because the body was simply meant as a vessel for the human's relationship with God. Only the human spirit would have demanded something more for itself than being hungry or having restricted nourishment options. The idolatrous voice that was given control was still within the human spirit. On the other hand, an evolutionary body would have been less than content with the prospect of being hungry, to say the least. Evolution craves everything beneficial for the organism, and hunger would be quite central to an organism's survival. Thus, even in the case of something that seems to be a bodily desire the first humans could have submitted to in any scenario, having an evolutionary heritage within the flesh proves to be distinct from the traditional viewpoint.

Within the first humans there was a power swelling through their veins they could likely feel, but were helpless to understand until after the fall. Nature had been created through rampant organism glorification that had gone uncontested for millions of years until the creation of humans. It is at the point of human creation that the raging stream of evolution was held back by the human spirit, and it would be foolishness to think the first humans did not feel this force with the weight of eons behind it pressing up against the will of their spirits. The idolatrous voice of evolution had been subdued, but was far from silent. All they needed to do was give this voice priority above God.

If a metaphorical interpretation of the tree in the garden is supposed, the route to giving an evolutionary flesh priority could have taken on variable appearances in nature around them. Perhaps eating the fruit was not the only way for them to sin and choose their flesh above God. To them, any act of satisfying the flesh was all right by itself, but when those desires were elevated above the spirit and therefore their connection to God, a significant inversion was made. For example, sex would have been entirely wholesome in its own right because of the union God had made between them, but they obviously could have looked around to see how sex can take on consuming proportions in animals. In fact, the story's command not to eat the fruit of a certain tree in the garden may really be a symbolic representation of God telling them to not succumb to the consuming desires of the flesh. God specifically says that they may eat food to a large extent but not beyond a certain point (in the story, a specific tree) (Gen 2:16). Is this not a limitation in the desires of the flesh? God allows them to partake in the desires but not be ruled by them. Whether there was actually a tree is irrelevant, for in submitting to the flesh, they were choosing to give priority to the idolatrous voice of the flesh above their relationship with God. Indeed, every self-serving desire as empowered by evolution and genetic advantage is choosing one's own well-being instead of trusting God.

In eating the fruit, or submitting to any other action of the flesh, they were choosing their bodies above God. The idolatrous voice of the flesh was given authority over human life because they desired to be above God, and the power of evolution pulsing through the flesh was perceived to be their ticket. But they could have never possessed the knowledge of what actually constituted the foundation of the flesh. That is, until they became slaves to it. They willfully chose to hand the reigns of their lives over to the flesh, and God gave them exactly what they requested. From that point forward, human flesh would have authority over the spirit. It was an earth-shaking inversion. The human spirit that had been created in reflection of God, the all-encompassing authority of nature, was enslaved by the medium for existence meant to be a mere servant. Humans were condemned to existence apart from God because the spirit is unable to reach God, trapped within the principles that constructed the flesh.

It is crucial to understand how this is distinct from any simple evolutionary Christian scenario, and especially how it maintains a flesh that is not evil. First, with regard to the previous analogy, it would be as if the person never got black paint on his or her clothing, but only put the black jacket back on. And not just a jacket, but also black pants and a black hat, to the point where his or her whole body was covered with black clothing. As a consequence of this dress style, the person is unable to enter, say, a certain social club, even though the person underneath is not dyed with black. The supremacy of the flesh is the entirety, not just a particular aspect, of our condemnation, and it banished us from the presence of God.

In regard to evil not being intrinsic to nature, a more complex analogy may help. Consider an entirely imagined scenario in which there are two groups: a royal family and a distinct entity of "heathens." The royal family lives completely differently from the heathens, solely because the royals are completely unique beings. The actions of the heathens cannot be considered evil because they are simply acting in the only way possible for them. It is important to understand that the characters in this scenario are not confined within human morals as their titles suggest. Suppose the members of the royal family wanted to overthrow the far-off king, so they gave authority to the heathens because they were led to believe it could increase their power. The authority was nothing the heathens could have seized on their own. The plan to overthrow the king fails, and as a result the royal family is tossed out among the heathens, never to escape their society. Is the royal family justified in now believing that the heathens are evil because they have been condemned to forever embody their practices? Clearly not, for the heathens were not evil before, and the foolish decision of the royal family does not change that fact. Rather, the circumstance of a royal family sequestered among heathens is severely evil, because royalty is meant for much higher aspirations.

Such is the situation of humanity. The flesh and its foundation of natural selection was never evil. The fact that the principles of the flesh now testify to our distance from God does not change this fact. Our spirits were meant to be blessed with a physical body while maintaining authority over its workings so that we can give complete glory to God. The loss of this ability is not the fault of the flesh, for we would have eventually betrayed God without any influence of the flesh. Although our separation from God is marked by the consuming desires of the flesh, we have no one to blame for their consuming power except ourselves and the Deceiver.

Doesn't all of this imply that there is a struggle going on between the spirit and the flesh? There must be an inherent conflict between the material body and immaterial spirit of the human being. But the long-standing Christian position has been that humans are holistic creatures, and rightfully so. We are not two distinct entities glued together and easily separated; rather, we are a body deeply infused and entangled with a spirit. To say that somehow the body would be tempting the spirit would assume that these entities have been separated. Surely the genetic selfishness of the flesh could only be a temptation for the spirit if the flesh was not inherently part of the spirit. Returning to the previous analogy, even though the "heathens" are not considered evil does not mean there is no conflict with the royal family due to an inability to combine two distinct entities.

As much as it would appear as though the body and the spirit need to be at odds for the human being to rebel against God through the glorification of genetic selfishness, the conclusion is not that simple. Consider the previously maintained belief that the human body was fashioned directly by God. In such a situation, there is an absence of any conflict. Material existence does not rub negatively against the immaterial existence on its own. So even in the case where we are a product of evolution, the vast majority of operating procedures within the human body remain unchanged and the body has no reason to be in conflict with the spirit. Yet, the caveat is introduced when considering the purpose behind the material existence in nature, or at least what nature sets as its purpose. Genetic selfishness affects the body by affirming its ultimate purpose on the earth; it does not directly alter the current state of the body itself (although it gives insight as to its workings).

For the most part, the body and the spirit have no grounds for being in conflict. When the body and the spirit were united in humans, it was a smooth union, except for an extra piece of baggage the body brought. The superficial purpose by which the body was created (genetic selfishness) did not effortlessly blend with the spirit. How could it? How could a sovereign spirit with complete freedom be compatible with selfish desires to constantly produce more genes? So, this additional caveat of physical existence needed to be tucked away and forgotten. If human beings are like homes, then genetic selfishness is a small, boarded-up room in the corner of the attic. The physical structure of the house and the essence of the people dwelling within it blend beautifully to make a home. There is no need to formulate a conflict between the walls and the homeowners. Yet, in the small, boarded-up room in the attic, the people are forbidden. This is where the conflict lies. They sense that there is something powerful locked away in that room, and it draws them to break in and seize this new knowledge. The human body is not in conflict with the human spirit such that they are forced to become two distinct entities. The body is neutral on its own; it is the means by which it was created that is dangerous. Genetic selfishness is baggage brought into the human person by the body and locked away from the first humans such that they could be completely free. But, they were tempted to pursue this alternate purpose and fell away from God because of something that was brought to them through physical existence.

Scripture repeatedly discusses the corrupted state of the human spirit bound by the sinful nature. Although an evolutionary perspective does not radically alter these truths, it seems to shed a more profound light on them, as outlined in the previous discussion. In describing the wrath of God against humankind, Paul states that those who abandoned the truth of God "worshiped and served created things rather than the Creator" (Rom 1:25).

This is in the midst of God giving people over to the desires of sexual immorality, implying that humans decided to worship their bodies and elevate physical desires above a pursuit of God. "Created things" is not simply nature itself, for are not humans much more prone to be absorbed with abilities of their created bodies rather than creation in general? Such a viewpoint is enlightened by evolution, which affirms that serving the flesh above God is not simply an example of sin in this particular situation, but the entire essence of the sinful nature. When God let people wallow in their sin, as illustrated in Romans 1, He was placing the flesh in complete authority over them, resulting in a mind deprived of thoughts of God (1:28) and a passion for everything selfish (1:29).

In other places, Paul describes enemies of the Gospel as having a god that is the stomach and a mind on earthly things (Phil 3:18), the wicked as seeking gratification for the cravings of the sinful nature (Eph 2:3), and the hard of heart as giving themselves over to the indulgence of impure sensuality (Eph 4:18). These examples illustrate a pattern in which sinful acts have connections with the physical body. Stomachs, cravings, and sensuality all convey sin as relating to the descriptions of life in the flesh. This is not entirely new, for a traditional framework would suppose the body and spirit are intertwined such that the desires of the spirit are the same as those of the flesh. So proposing that the human body craves something is equivalent to proposing that the spirit craves something. But the fact that each of these depictions of sin points directly to the workings of the flesh is expected from an evolutionary viewpoint. The sinful nature is rooted in the flesh, and although that does not nullify the spirit's partaking in its activities, these quintessential displays of life apart from God stem from the flesh and the desires ingrained by evolution. Scripture depicts slavery to sin as a battle with the flesh. Evolution would support this notion while emphasizing that the flesh is the entire source of these chains; the spirit has nothing to do with the cravings of sin other than its original submission.

Acting outside of the flesh is impossible without God. We chose to become animals again, and now the pursuits of the flesh have us in chains. This is the central difference evolution makes to the events of the fall that unfolded in the garden. We were not simply choosing to distrust God; we were elevating the self-glorifying desires of our flesh to the point that our actions reverted us back to the position of an animal. We put the satisfaction of the medium ahead of the life of the spirit, a place it had no business being, and the result was submersion back into the control of the medium (the flesh). Our motive for this course of action was essentially a mutiny against God. We desired to overthrow the King and put ourselves in His place, and the power of the flesh seemed like our means to do so. The rebellion failed, and we became slaves to the evolutionary heritage that we had given authority. Now, our separation from God is displayed by the qualities of the evolutionary flesh, not because it is evil, but because it is the quintessential mode through which the human spirit is separated from God, and that separation is deeply evil

SIDE EFFECTS OF SLAVERY

At this point, any reasonable person is beginning to question the wide-sweeping definitions that have been made thus far. The previously discussed scenario postulates that our sinful nature is defined by the desires ingrained within our flesh, because it is the authority of the flesh that separates us from God. It would seem as though everything about the sinful nature should be connected to evolution. Yet, it does not take much examination to notice that this is highly questionable. We know from experience that life separated from God has several qualities that are hardly connected to evolutionary desires. Even if the sinful nature to a large extent is drawn upon by evolution, it seems unwarranted to propose that our separation from God is entirely due to the dominion of the flesh if it is unable to account for all levels of human brokenness.

Throughout a day, there are any number of thoughts entering the human mind. Many of them have evolutionary connection. For example, one could be lusting for sex, jealous of his or her neighbor, brewing over bad blood, or strategizing how to acquire material pleasure/power. But there are a number of other, more subtle thoughts that have no direct evolutionary connection: I am ashamed of my past. There's no hope for me. Am I loved? I have no purpose. My weaknesses control me. Not only is there no evolutionary reason for thoughts like these (and perhaps actually disadvantage), they are also traditionally characterized as the work of Satan. If Satan has already been established as deceiving humans by working through the flesh, what are we to make of these thoughts that are familiar to so much of humanity?

Although it may seem problematic that a significant aspect of our distance from God is not connected to the heritage of our flesh, realistically consider the situation of a human spirit bound within flesh. As soon to be discussed (see the section "The Distinction"), the human spirit does have a small amount of inconsequential freedom within the flesh. How would we expect the human spirit to act when it begins to show its presence from within the strangle-hold of the flesh? Obviously, not in a particularly truthful manner. So it is unsurprising there are untruthful thoughts that pertain to the spiritual realm in the human mind. Even though we have thoughts that are indicative of our distance from God and have no evolutionary connection, they are nonetheless a consequence of bondage to the flesh.

Consider those unique vehicles that can operate as both a car and a boat. They have wheels to move on land and a propeller to cut through the water. Now, imagine one of these vehicles in the middle of the ocean. Its mode of transportation becomes entirely one-dimensional. But what happens if the wheels begin to spin as if it were on land? It may inch forward slowly, although not in a manner resembling its abilities on land. As long as it is stuck in the middle of the ocean, the wheels will be useless. In a similar manner, as long as the human spirit is trapped within the flesh, its efforts will be primarily unsuccessful. The thoughts in the human spirit can "spin," but the aptitude to reason correctly will be severely limited due to the surrounding environment.

Satan, the great deceiver, is typically seen as the direct source of these untruthful thoughts, and this is no less significant. Separation from God results in thoughts such as these, with distance from God tracing back to Satan. He is still separating us from God, but in a way that seems deceptively intrinsic to who we are: the flesh. That which is viewed as the central pillar of human existence is far from benign as a result of Satan tempting us to misplace its ultimate authority. Being far from God in the control of Satan is still the reason we have thoughts that are untruthful; the only difference is that the separation from God takes the specific form of being bonded within the flesh.

An equivalent idea can be applied to the actions that pertain to the spiritual realm. What connection does sin such as witchcraft, idolatry, or false prophets have to do with evolution? Is there any potential genetic advantage for those who practice witchcraft, or erect statues of idols, or lead people from the path of righteousness? They certainly don't seem to be connected to evolution. Acts such as these appear to stem directly from the moral crookedness of the human spirit apart from the flesh. But this conception is misguided because of the assumption it invokes.

In questioning whether the crookedness of the spirit can be the source of a particular sinful action, it is once again implied that the flesh would have no effect on the spirit. When the spirit reasons on spiritual matters, it is assumed to make independent decisions. But the flesh has a strangling influence on the spirit. When it seems as though humans are directly rebellious to God in a spiritual manner, it must be remembered that a human spirit made distant from God in the flesh is not likely to act righteously in spiritual matters because of that same flesh. Even when it appears to be a spiritual chess match, the flesh could in fact be the influence that moves the pieces. Human spirits are not crooked in and of themselves; they are in an immoral situation because of the flesh. That does not insinuate an evil flesh, but that a spirit enslaved within the flesh is an evil situation.

But there is an additional caveat here. Satan is the root of all evil, and while his vastly favorite tool is the flesh, it is not the only one he uses. Even though the human spirit is not usually the root for sin, this does not mean spiritual sin is nonexistent. Satan has no flesh dragging him down, but he nonetheless is distant spiritually from God. So it is possible that at times Satan directly addresses the spirit and tries to convince it to follow his lead. In other words, our spirits are usually dragged into sin by the flesh, but there may be circumstances in which the spirit chooses to sin directly through a reflection of Satan's spiritual fall. A few human spirits are tempted into becoming intrinsically evil by Satan, but most of them are condemned only because the flesh is in authority. Consider the fall in the garden. Although we chose to trust the flesh over God, this does not imply a directly spiritual rebellion as present in Satan and his followers. But at the same time, there is still the possibility that Satan could cultivate this same hatred of God in the human spirit. Based on human experience, though, it seems Satan much prefers to tempt us through the flesh. Therefore, some actions of directly spiritual sin could be due to an evil spirit, although most are rooted in a flesh that keeps the spirit from considering spiritual matters truthfully.

WHY SO NARROW?

Why does genetic selfishness have to be the defining aspect of our separation from God? Most people at this point would have no problem acknowledging that the principles of existence laid down by evolution are clearly detrimental to the human being as fashioned by God. An obsession with one's well-being through the propagation of genes is obviously not part of God's plan for us. But why does it have to be the cornerstone of our rebellion against God? He designed us for a specific purpose among creation, and we decided to forsake this purpose and fell away from our relationship with Him. The scenario postulated earlier states that this rebellion against God took the specific form of glorifying the genetically selfish principles of the flesh, and the other aspects of separation from God came along as a result of this. Yet, couldn't the genetic selfishness of the flesh simply be one of many ways that we rebel against God? Surely, something that maintains an inherent selfishness must be an act against God, but humans are certainly capable of doing other things that separate them from God. Why can't genetic selfishness simply be one of many aspects of human rebellion?

Although there is nothing wrong with an alternate scenario such as this, it fails to grasp the gravity of the selfish foundation in our bodies. To begin, it can first be pointed out that a significant portion of human sinfulness has a strong evolutionary connection. Many of our actions that are contrary to God's plan for us would be justified in a purely evolutionary environment. This should hardly be surprising, for evolution is built upon

47

selfishness, which is a defining aspect, if not the foundation, of human sinfulness. So, it is only reasonable to suppose that submitting to the genetic selfishness of evolution is the defining aspect of human rebellion against God, because it is vastly the most palpable characteristic of human sinfulness.

Examining our current state gives adequate reason for defining genetic selfishness as the route of our fall from God, but considering the situation of the first humans only furthers this objective. Water that is flowing to the ocean will always take the path of least resistance, and humans typically mirror this pattern. If someone has an objective, the easiest path is the preferred route, although there are exceptions. Imagine the first humans as walking with God down a path in the forest, and rebellion takes the form of running off the path into the forest. Obviously, there are numerous ways this could happen. But what if there was already another path leading off into the forest? If leaving the original path in an act of defiance against God is the goal, an existing path would be an undeniable preference. And how much more would this effect be compounded if it was not some overgrown side path, but a well-worn path traversed by every organism ever to exist? Living in bodies built under the purpose of selfishness meant we had a readily accessible way to rebel against God based on an alternate purpose that had not been questioned over its eons of reign. True, it is only a superficial purpose, and animals never had any choice but to travel that path. But once we were given the opportunity to have a higher purpose in relationship with God, it is not difficult to see why a rebellion against Him would be accomplished by submitting to the selfishness already present in our flesh. When considering the fall of the first humans (and our repeated falls), it is fully reasonable to suppose that the selfishness that created our bodies was the defining route of our fall.

THE MOTIVE

If considering the possibility that the flesh is the source of our separation from God has not been dumbfounding, considering why God chose to create humanity in this way likely will be. God does not act haphazardly, so the question obviously becomes why God intentionally designed humans to possess an evolutionary flesh. Why did He create humans from a natural world that is intrinsically selfish if He knew humans would one day be enslaved by the same principles of nature in their flesh? It could be supposed that God simply had to make do with what He had at the end of evolution, but this is quite unsatisfying in the providence of God. On the other hand, it is difficult to propose that God could have created a human society with just the human soul. Our existence was always meant to have a physical aspect to it. And yet, it was still entirely within His power to make a human body from scratch without billions of years of selfish genetic glorification.

Within the consideration of God willfully choosing the bodies of humans to be made by evolution, the temptation that glorification of the flesh provided to the first humans can be addressed. Although it must be maintained that humans would have turned away from God even in a genetically neutral body, what does evolutionary bodies add to the equation? On the surface, it seems like an entirely destructive situation, because temptation would be much stronger when the spirit is thoroughly intertwined with a body made to do the opposite of God's will. If God truly desired above all that we follow Him, wouldn't an easier path have been better? Certainly. But His goal is not our pursuit of Him *above all*, for ultimately we were created for the glory of God (Eph 1:12).

God is given more glory when beings with free will choose to follow Him even in the face of forceful opposition to the very fiber of their constitution. The fish that swims upstream is much more remarkable than one that simply swims around in a lake. When free will is combined with an intense inclination built over millions of years to glorify oneself, the choice to follow God brings Him exceedingly more glory. Still, the fact that the events did not turn out this way is irrelevant, for this indulges in the difficult topic of God's providence that is beyond our grasp. All we can affirm is that God planned for us to fall and for His Son to save us. How this brings Him the maximum amount of glory is incomprehensible.

However, there is another aspect of a sinful nature tied to an evolutionary flesh that is interesting to consider. It is difficult to understand and partially speculative, but it could provide a significant payoff when considering God's motive in human evolution. Why we became slaves to sin needs to be considered. Obviously, sinning means we will always miss the perfection of God, but does that necessarily imply that we should fall all the way into slavery? If the human spirit is prone to distrust God apart from the desires of the evolutionary flesh present to provide temptation, then we would have always missed a relationship with God. But to say that we would automatically come under the complete control of evil desires seems like an overstepping of the situation. In creatures with free will, failing to comply with the perfection of God should not nullify any desire to be connected with God. And yet, we became slaves to sin without any ability to seek God apart from the work of the Holy Spirit. Why should this be? Why would beings with free will suddenly be removed of any ability to merely seek God on their own?

Considering the human situation in comparison to that of fallen angels such as Satan may be helpful in this regard. Both angels and humans have turned away from God, and yet, only humans have a redemption plan for a return to God. It would be easy to simply chalk the whole situation up to the unexplainable grace of God, and although this is reasonable, it is not useful for the present discussion. In examining the situation in more detail, it is first realized that Satan and his companions have never been slaves to anything. They are continually choosing to be against God, as opposed to humans who are unable to have any thought of God on their own because they are slaves to sin. But what exactly does that mean? How are we slaves to sin? If it resulted simply because the human spirit turned against God, then the situation would be no different from that of Satan, for the human spirit chose to become intrinsically evil.

Perhaps a highly imaginative analogy will help. Imagine that God dwells in Europe with angels around Him. Some of the angels decided to rebel against Him and move to North America. Whether they chose to move or were forced to is irrelevant, because it is much like when someone gets fed up with his or her boss and explodes in the boss's face. The employee is surely fired, but he or she was on the way out anyway. Where this does become important in the present analogy is in the fact that Satan and the fallen angels have no way to make it back to Europe from North America. Still, they fully know that Europe exists, and they hate God's presence there. While they are technically unable to return, they would nevertheless refuse the opportunity to do so because of a complete resentment of God. Now, suppose there are other beings in, say, South America. God draws them near to His presence, and with Holy reverence they almost lose every concept of the millennia they spent on their mother continent. While there, however, they choose (with the provoking of Satan) to forsake their new citizenship in Europe and give priority to their older citizenship in South America. As a result, God ships them back to South America, from which they can no longer return to Europe. Yet, their situation is different from Satan's, for they are returning to a previously native country. They are not there solely to get away from God, as in the case of Satan in North America. They are there because they chose a "previous citizenship" over God. And because it was not purely running away from God, these beings become entrenched in the previous way of life. There is not even a mere thought of Europe, but only blissful blindness to what lies beyond.

Such is the situation of humanity from an evolutionary perspective. We were not created in neutral bodies sculpted by the hand of God. If we had been, our situation would be no different from that of Satan, for there would have been no heritage for our reversion of citizenship. Any turning against God would have been a spiritual rebellion that hinged upon our trusting the deepest part of our being. It would have been like God creating the beings directly in Europe, and then those beings running off to start a country of their own. Importantly, the mind-set of the humans indeed was to independently start their own country, but that's not how it worked out. They did not know it, but in rebelling against God, they were actually returning to slavery in a previous country rather than staking an independent lot.

So we can now begin to answer those troubling questions. First, why was our free will partially removed? Simply put, because we were returning to the dominion of a previous country. Satan was not going back to anything, and his capacity for action with or against God theoretically was not restricted. Humans chose to make their physical existence a priority (in an attempt to unseat God, no less), and they became bound within a physical existence, unable to have any thought of God. If we had simply rebelled against God in a manner identical to that of Satan (as traditionally supposed), then slavery to a sinful life that is unable to acknowledge God is somewhat difficult to understand in a logical manner.

Second, and back to the original question, why did God set up the scenario in such a fashion? In essence, God gave us a depth to fall that would be rescuable. Think of it like a parent who places their child on top of a high hill and tells the child not to jump off. The parent knows the child will jump anyway, so the parent devises a system. On one side of the hill there is a cliff that plunges to jagged rocks below, but on the other side of the hill there is a gentler slope, although still rough. In such a scenario, the child is able to rebel and jump off the hill and not be entirely decimated by the jagged rocks, because there is another option. The child surely is in terrible shape when he or she reaches the bottom and has no capacity to return to the top, but the child is not entirely razed. God gave us a way to fall from Him that was distinct from the route of Satan so that somehow He could save us. Importantly, we are no closer to God than Satan is when we become slaves to the flesh. Both actions deserve nothing but death. But there is some way in which our position is actually rescuable.

All of the simplistic analogies of our relationship to God and the corresponding placement of Satan appear to make light of our distance from God, as if it wasn't so bad after all. This could not be further from the truth. God's redemptive actions are absolutely remarkable. We spat in His face by choosing a mere physical flesh over His presence. And yet, He drudged down to the bottom of that hill to lift us from the quagmire in which we had landed. There was no way back up to Him without His help. We would have remained there in death indefinitely. It was no farther away from Him than Satan had fallen, but there was still a sense in which we had hope after a uniquely different fall—not because we could even dream of lifting ourselves back up again, but because our spirits had not been annihilated on the way down. Still, they were tarnished with filth and bent in grotesque ways. That a perfectly clean God would stoop down to clean up that mess is incomprehensible.

FREEDOM

Each one of us is born into slavery. We come into this world controlled by the flesh, unable to even ponder the divine. Animals have no ability to think of God, and when the original humans gave the flesh priority, we became like every other animal. This necessarily brings up two important questions. Why do humans not appear like every other animal? And how are we individually culpable for a rebellion against God if we are simply born into the results of that rebellion? The first of these questions will be dealt with a bit later, although it has the same answer as the second question, to be dealt with presently.

General revelation, as given by God, fundamentally alters the entire scenario of our slavery. We know from the Bible that God reveals Himself to everyone, such that no one is without excuse for denying Him. So what does this look like for slavery? As we toil away with our burdens in the flesh, He comes along to give us an inkling that escape may be possible. It's not explicit, and it looks overwhelmingly difficult, yet even a glimpse of paradise is more than we deserve. Bestowed with this privilege, any return to our toils of slavery is nothing short of a reenactment of humanity's original rebellion. We have no excuse for our present state of slavery, for the merciful hand from heaven was extended, and we willing turned away.

How this general revelation from God was used to escape slavery for generations of ancient humans will be dealt with in due time (see the section "Salvation"). But the more pressing topic is what freedom from slavery looks like and how we attain it today. If the flesh is the source of our chains, then liberation must imply a rescue of the spirit from the flesh. To escape slavery, individuals must remove themselves from the source of their slavery. At least that's how we usually imagine it. Surely, this is a potential solution to our problem. Completely liberating the spirit from the flesh would theoretically resolve our separation from God. But that's not the solution God has in mind. In escaping slavery, there are two options: One can either run away from his or her captors or overcome them. Running away is certainly the easier option. And yet, God never intended for us to live without the flesh. Our captors are not a separate entity to escape but an important part of who we were always meant to be as humans. The flesh was central to the purpose of human existence from the beginning, although it was never meant to be the dominant authority in human life.

So in coming to be freed from the flesh, we are additionally not attempting to throw the flesh into the garbage heap of society. Consider the humans in the garden. They must have partaken in some pleasures of the flesh, such as eating, exercising, and union between a husband and wife. So God does not wish for physical existence to be completely absent at this time from what it means to live as a human. But He most surely desires that the body is put in its rightful place, which is second. C. S. Lewis once described how we will never be able to get "second things" by putting them first; only by putting "first things" first will we be able to receive "second things." In its original context, this taught that the possessions of this world were never meant to be a priority, and making them a priority will often negate their acquisition. Only by putting God first does everything else fall into its rightful place. Does this not describe the entire situation of the human race from an evolutionary perspective? We chose to place the secondary satisfaction of the body above the spiritual relationship with God, a place it had no business being. The flesh needs to return to a secondary position for God to be reseated at His rightful place in human lives.

In coming to know God again, we are not completely abandoning everything pertaining to the flesh. Rather, we are placing it where it was designed to be in the beginning. We learn to control the body in a way that is holy and not bound within the passionate lusts of humanity (1 Thess 4:5).

In fact, we would expect that the actions of the flesh would be enjoyed in a much more fulfilling sense when under the circumstances intended, thus resulting in a significantly different perspective on the actions of everyday life by someone set free from the flesh. What was once an absolute need becomes a privilege to enjoy. Our relationship with God is deeply spiritual; anything done in the flesh beyond what is necessary to keep the body alive to worship God is simply an opportunity to experience the other aspects of human existence. Pursuits of the body were never meant to bear the entire weight of a human spirit. Rather, the body is able to thrive under the lessened pressure when the spirit becomes connected to God. Those freed from the flesh possess a higher perspective whether they realize it or not, and even the events of day-to-day life become significantly different in nature.

With this in mind, we can return to the consideration of sex and its connection to the flesh. Traditionally, sex within a marriage is viewed as a gift from God, but if partaking in the acts of the flesh means turning away from God, how can it be that God not only approves of it but celebrates satisfaction of the flesh in this context? Obviously, in some sense, God had to allow sex if the human race was to continue, but that does not explain why it would be celebrated. Perhaps the idea that sex is a gift from God is entirely erroneous. In that case, allowing sex in the context of marriage is simply a compromise between the continuity of the human race and abstaining from self-glorification through the desires of evolution. Yet, maybe there is another way God uses sex, even though it is a dirty pleasure in its origin.

The physical pleasure surely cannot have a direct connection to God, for evolution would have played a strong part in formulating this pleasure. But He could very well use this intense pleasure to affect the soul in a powerful way. Could there really be any better route to form a strong bond and intimate relationship between two people? In that case, sex is a gift only through the intimacy it creates when the act is done in two bodies housing a spirit. The physical pleasure has nothing to do with God except for the fact that it has been at work throughout evolution and has now only been co-opted to serve a new function. Partaking in the flesh within the context of marriage must not remove God from His throne, at least not in the ideal sense, because it is not considered absolutely sinful. In the context of marriage joined by God, the extremely powerful desires of the flesh are systematically restrained in such a way as to ensure that they remain in a secondary position compared to God. This may not always work out ideally in society, but the allowing of sex within a marriage illustrates how desires of the flesh can be satisfied as long as they are of a far subordinate priority compared with God.

It cannot be too quickly added that this is a slippery slope. Partaking in the actions of the flesh results in pleasure of some variety, and this pleasure, which is much more tangible than the presence of God, can force itself back into a priority position very easily. It can be entirely subtle, for the spirit can be convinced it is still honoring God above everything else, but the flesh may be calling the shots in reality. The constant difficulty comes by way of the fact that human existence convincingly seems inseparably linked to pleasures of the body. It is the general perception that actions of the flesh are entirely innocent, and we can enjoy them to any extent as long as God is still within the mix somewhere, because He will always come out as the priority. But this is not true. Actions of the flesh are risky. Billions of years of selection have built the body on a foundation of selfishness, and to say that these pleasures can be mindlessly indulged is Satan's way of removing God from a position of authority.

This is where an evolutionary perspective offers very powerful insight. By first labeling the flesh as the temptation for selfishness that pulled us away from God and erected a sinful nature, the true identity of the body is unmasked. The caution that the human spirit may choose to turn away from God becomes a fear that the human spirit may be led away from God by the pleasures of the flesh. It is as if we become aliens in our bodies. We can partake in its pleasures, but there is a constant reminder that our bodies should not be deemed innocent at this time. Thus, an evolutionary perspective more accurately pinpoints the force that is driving us away from God. It is not necessarily a quality of the human spirit to run away on its own from that which can give life. It is being tempted to turn away from God by that which is always begging for authority. Indeed, this is a perplexing situation in need of God's grace. We are called to enjoy the pleasures of life, but those very same pleasures are constantly in the business of tempting us away from God.

Let us return to the scenario of a royal family sequestered in a society of heathens. If the royal family was given the opportunity to be freed from heathen society and be reconnected with the king, how would they then perceive the heathen society? In the case that their freedom is not immediately complete, their perception of the heathens is crucial. How the royal family relates to their captors will influence the degree to which they can rekindle a relationship with the king. As long as they live in heathen society they will be required to follow its practices, but how they relate to these practices is vital. Remember that the heathens themselves were not evil; the supremacy of heathen society over the royal family was evil. So escaping this evil will require overcoming the addictive culture that has enslaved them, while still remaining in that culture. It is a delicate maneuver. Haphazardly living within heathen society will undoubtedly lead to being controlled by the practices of that culture, which have become deeply pleasurable to them. Members of the royal family must be weary of the heathen society if they are to partake in, and even enjoy, their culture while not being ruled by it. If humans are to escape the suffocating authority of the flesh, our physical pleasures need to be considered less than benign.

As important as it is to consider what Godly freedom from the flesh appears like, it is infinitely more important to understand the events that lead to this freedom being available to us today. And for that we turn to God's redemptive actions, which are foundational to all Christian thought. How do the redemptive actions of Jesus at the cross change from an evolutionary perspective? Jesus is still redeeming the human spirit from its choice to turn away from God. In that sense, he is still paying the penalty of the human spirit's decision to distrust God, but the nature of the penalty is somewhat different. Not only is separation from God a consequence of sin, but that separation takes the form of being chained within an animal. So, if being liberated to seek God means our penalty needs to be paid, Jesus paid the penalty that most characterizes the burdens of an animal: death.

To be sure, on the cross Jesus experienced complete spiritual separation from God the Father, but isn't this separation from God really what the human spirit chained within an animal is? By being chained within an animal, our spirits are separated from God, not by distance but by capability to seek Him. He is all around, and yet there is an insurmountable

58

wall that is constructed when the animal has complete authority over the spirit. Clearly, the separation is not fully cultivated until hell, and yet there is still a sense in which we can understand what happened at the cross because we struggle with it daily. Jesus chained himself in the prison of the flesh, although he had never submitted to it, and bore the central burden of every animal. Still, it was to a degree that we could never witness outside of hell and to an extent for all His followers that puts it beyond comprehension, but that does not lessen its reflection in the life we know. Separation from God is not something that has been delayed until death. We can already see signs of it in the bondage to the flesh. And this separation would have only continued if God would not have been present among people to open their eyes even before the coming of Christ. Thus, if the sinful nature is linked to the flesh, then Jesus did not simply take on flesh in the sense that he was in a human body; he endured the weight of punishment for what it meant to be chained within flesh: separation from God.

It can also be considered why Satan is vanquished specifically because of what Jesus did and not simply because God decided to destroy him by His power. Satan is removed from his influence on the flesh because a man who did not deserve the bondage and separation from God characteristic of the flesh bore the penalty anyway and overcame it. Specifically, overcoming death is what uprooted Satan from his position of influence over the flesh. We were thrown under the influence of Satan through the bodies we toil with, and the only path to liberation was for God to punish someone else under the burdens of the flesh who did not deserve it so that he could subsequently overcome it. Through death, the most certain pain of existence in the flesh, Jesus was handed over to Satan. By rising again, he conquered the flesh, and abolished Satan's reign in the mortal bodies. From that day forward, Satan's days of torturing the human spirit through the flesh were numbered, and one day they will come to an end.

How does this change our experience? The fact that Jesus saved our spirits from the penalty of distrusting God is the same. What changes is the nature of that penalty. He bore what we have already been struggling with for tens of thousands of years in the slavery to the flesh, although he never succumbed to it. So our experience of having the penalty paid and life freed from the flesh are one in the same. This creates a cohesive picture in the death of Christ and our freedom from sin. By recognizing that Christ was not simply suffering what may have been reserved for us in hell, but the burdens of slavery to flesh we experience every day, we can more fully ponder freedom. Hell is not our only punishment for distrusting God; becoming a slave to a flesh that is overflowing with the sinful nature is our punishment.

The sinful nature is usually assumed to cause the penalty of death, but it is actually our punishment for rebellion (which necessarily includes death), delivered by slavery to flesh. Jesus suffered this slavery to flesh that results in spiritual death through separation from God, and now we need not succumb to it any longer. The penalty due us in spiritual death through supreme flesh has been paid by Jesus. When the sinful nature is centered on the evolutionary body, it becomes clear that Jesus did not die to save our spirits from an inclination to distrust God, but from a flesh that refuses to glorify God. His death did not reform the human spirit, as supposed when the sinful nature is a quality of the spirit, but set it free from the flesh that invokes the constant need to glorify oneself. It would be irresponsible on our part to continue believing the flesh is an innocent medium for the existence of the human spirit, because in reality, dominion to flesh is the penalty Jesus paid.

THE MINISTRY OF JESUS

His Followers

The people who felt drawn to Jesus were not the most upstanding members of society. On multiple occasions he befriends tax collectors (Mk 2:14; Lk 19:5) along with a variety of other "sinners" (Mt 9:9). Likely among them was a following of prostitutes. The people of Jesus' public ministry were all the types of people who were looked down upon in that society. Not only that, but his inner circle consisted of people not much higher on the social hierarchy. They were working men of humble origins who toiled for their day-to-day sustenance. The force of Jesus' message was felt most strongly by a unique group of people, and an examination of the reasons for this with consideration of evolution proves insightful.

Jesus' message attracted those who were lowest in society. It could be supposed that these people were already humble and were therefore more receptive to the coming of a new King than those who were prideful, but it goes deeper than that. The majority of these people had insignificant material power (aside from tax collectors) and were considered outcasts among the community. Now consider human evolution. In a group of evolving hominids (hominids, like apes, are community animals), what factors would contribute most to the amount of sex an individual partook in? Clearly, material power and community status were enormously significant. The individual with the greatest amount of resources under his domain received the most sex, and the individual who was an authoritative figure usually took control of sexual claims. Being ostracized from the community was a genetic death wish. The outcasts died without passing on any genetic heritage because any other community would be highly distrusting of outsiders.

The people most drawn to Jesus lacked that which was most vital in human evolution. Their genetic heritage was likely minimal, if existent at all. What does this mean? In essence, the power of their flesh was naturally being suffocated. If the desires of evolution for genetic heritage are a raging beast in each person, the beast in these people was being starved. What their genes wanted most was being repeatedly thwarted. This is significant because they were receptive to the preaching of Jesus, which commanded a forsaking of these principles. They were prepared to kill the beast of the flesh because the beast was already weak from a lack of positive feedback.

Hominid evolution involved communities that likely had a resemblance to ape communities today, so it is useful to draw a parallel. Imagine Jesus coming to a tribe of chimpanzees or gorillas in which there is a rigidly enforced hierarchy. He did not come to approach the alpha male and convince him not only that his leadership has been superseded, but also that this whole system of hierarchal living is worthless. Obviously, it would do no good. So Jesus came to appeal to the lowest in the community. He came to reach out to the subordinate chimp who is routinely beaten by superiors and is trapped within the most disadvantageous position. Someone who preaches escape from this system that was readily produced by the constructs of genetic selfishness would be quickly accepted, even if escape necessitates rising above rather than fleeing. The people of Jesus' ministry were most receptive to a lifestyle that included abandoning the authority of the flesh because they were already living in a situation in which the flesh was being sapped of its most fundamental feedstocks.

This can equally be seen in the statements of blessing and woe made by Jesus. Those who find favor in his Kingdom are the poor, hungry, mournful, and hated because of allegiance to him (Lk 6:20-22), whereas an unfavorable position is bestowed upon the rich, well fed, laughing, and widely accepted (Lk 6: 24-26). For Jesus, those who would be most receptive to his coming Kingdom were those with the greatest evolutionary disadvantage. Material riches, physical strength, and community acceptance were to be fiercely pursued, and mourning likely meant having the community ravaged in battle with neighboring tribes. All of these factors resulted in less genetic heritage, and living with the constant burden of them caused a person to develop a numbness to the influence of evolution. The selfish power within the flesh was not being positively reinforced by the circumstances of life. This left a person receptive to a message that, among other things, included a forsaking of the chains humanity had found in the flesh.

His Temptation

The temptation of Jesus in the wilderness provides insight into the movements of Satan in relation to the flesh. The first of these temptations was to miraculously create food to satisfy overwhelming starvation (Mt 4:3), the second to test God (4:6), and the third to bow down to Satan (4:9). Satan's progression of temptation is significant because it consistently mirrors human experience. The foremost technique used by Satan is temptation through the flesh. Forty days without food, and the evolutionary heritage of Jesus was screaming for nourishment. Satan's first route to corrupting Jesus was to use the power of the flesh, just as he had done to the first humans. However, once Jesus proved to have conquered the temptation of the flesh, Satan progressed from merely physical submission to spiritual rebellion in testing God and worshiping Satan. In this progression, two important insights result.

Why are the workings of Satan synonymous with the flesh? The first of Jesus' temptations exemplifies the primary route of corrupting human life. Both through the fall and in our everyday lives, we are deceived by Satan to glorify the selfish workings of the flesh above God. Why does Satan choose such a route? He may not be all-knowing, but it doesn't take much insight to realize that the best way to corrupt people is by using something that is rooted deeply within them. Satisfying the body feels indistinguishable from satisfying the spirit, so indulging the flesh must be permissible if our spirits are to receive their satisfaction and be filled with life. But fulfillment of the spirit is distinct, and predominantly contrary, to satisfaction of the selfish power within the flesh. Satan uses what is already present within our human bodies to achieve maximum deception and pull us away from God. Using what seems to be an entirely innocent and deeply ingrained piece of our being makes misplacement of the ultimately supremacy of our lives practically automatic.

Although Satan's favorite tool is the flesh, it is not his last resource. As exemplified in Jesus' later temptations, there is a purely spiritual realm of rebellion against God that is at his disposal. He is a being without flesh, which makes it obvious that rebellion against God does not necessitate glorifying the flesh. It is entirely possible for the human spirit to rebel against God in purely spiritual terms in a way parallel to that of Satan and delivered in a temptation similar to that of Jesus. When a person has been freed from the flesh, or has had the power of the flesh beaten to a pulp by life's circumstances, that individual then becomes a target for direct spiritual temptation. Obviously, those who have been freed from the slavery to the flesh by God are able to mount a strong resistance to such temptation. But those who have been beaten down by the constructs of human life in the flesh are in a dangerous situation. Those in human history who were considered "evil" on a deeper level than the general population usually lived through circumstances that left them mentally and emotionally damaged. As with the people of Jesus' ministry, the raging beast of the flesh had been crippled by life's circumstances, allowing the spirit some small, yet significant, amount of freedom. And without the Holy guidance of God, such a spirit is primed for unprecedented spiritual temptation by Satan.

His Healing

The healing ministry of Jesus is an interesting subject of examination, for it was essentially a reversal of the degradation central to evolution. He was known to heal lepers (Lk 5:13), paralytics (Mk 2:11), chronic bleeding (Mk 5:29), the deaf and mute (Mk 7:31), the blind (Lk 18:42), and any number of other health problems (Lk 4:40). All of these diseases are a natural part of an evolutionary environment. They can result from factors such as parasitic infection, genetic malfunction, and cellular death. It would be simple to suppose that Jesus was removing the burdens of suffering from the lives of people because breathing life was his ministry, but it is more complicated than that. He was ushering in the Kingdom of God and a physical existence that mirrored what was possible before the fall. So the question becomes: how was Jesus imparting the type of life possible before the fall?

Before the fall, the human spirit was in authority over the flesh.

Something about this situation must have nullified the controlling principles of nature. To be without death and able to live with God forever, the issues of health in the flesh must have been nonexistent. It doesn't seem to necessarily follow that a spirit in authority over the flesh would automatically remove any degradation of the flesh, but the source of our spirits is an important consideration. The spirits imparted to us are a reflection of Him, and just as it is ridiculous to suppose that God could be subject to disease, it could be the same situation with human spirits. With the spirit supreme over the flesh, humans were free from the principles of nature because they reflected the sovereign creator of nature. So before falling into slavery to the flesh, humans were without the burdens of degrading health.

If the healing of Jesus' ministry was a restoring of human life before the fall, then his healing included the liberation of the spirit above the flesh in some small sense. The person need not be completely made perfect, and completely free from the flesh, to be healed. All that was needed was a glimmer of the vibrantly healthy existence possible when the spirit is in authority for the effects of degradation to be reversed. Jesus' healing was less an external decree and more an internal rejuvenation. He was not imparting the perfection of God from the outside; he was sprouting perfection through an internal awakening only possible through the power of God. Healing meant a reestablishment of the spirit above the flesh, if only in some small sense.

His Preaching

As already touched on, the preaching of Jesus is in sharp contrast to the workings of evolution. The first subject this contrast pertains to how we are to interact with the constructs and possessions of the physical world. Jesus desires for us to relate to the physical world in a way that exemplifies a lack of power in the forces of evolution. Most obvious on this list is riches and the accumulation of wealth. Through an interaction with a wealthy young man, Jesus instructs that it is very difficult for the rich to enter the kingdom of God (Mt 19:16-30). The evolutionary connection is easy to spot, for an accumulation of material wealth weighed strongly on the possibility of sex for ancient hominids. It is not surprising that Jesus would state that those who are absorbed in an integral power of the flesh are far from the kingdom of God, which delivers freedom from the flesh and communion with God. Yet, Jesus does not require that we remove all material wealth from our lives; he simply commands that we must be vigilant to never be ruled by it, as exemplified in the parable of the rich fool (Lk 13-21). We can partake in the objects of this world, but we cannot find our identity in them, as would be automatic for an individual living in an entirely evolutionary environment. The flesh is persistent in convincing us that the wealth of the world is to be pursued at all costs, but we must ponder the reality beyond the flesh and restrain the inkling to be an animal consumed with this world (Mt 6:19-24).

The preaching of Jesus also claims an influence on the foundation of this world beyond wealth. He instructs that those who follow him may need to live without homes (Mt 8:20), leave family (Mt 10:37), and simply lose their entire lives (Mt 10:39). Surely, evolution would be appalled at the idea of releasing complete control of life. Genetic selfishness is built on the principle of unrelenting control of one's being. Living without a home, without a strong community, and without any claim to one's life runs straight in the face of evolution. Thus, obeying the commands of Jesus requires subduing the supremacy of the flesh and choosing to follow the Lord. He sends out his disciples on journeys to further his ministry without any provisions and tells them to trust him (Lk 9:3). We are to do the same: Forsake the desire to invest entirely in the provisions of this world, and trust that God will provide—an act no animal could ever dream of doing.

Naturally, discussion of trusting God for material provisions leads into a consideration of Jesus' teaching on worry. Jesus instructs that we should not worry about our food or clothing because the birds of the air and grasses of the field are sustained by God even though they do not worry, so He will certainly provide for us (Mt 6:25-34). Anyone with a working knowledge of evolution quickly realizes the statements of this passage appear contrary to reality. God is said to provide for birds, yet we know that birds are routinely dying. They must toil for their daily food, and often go without it until they starve to death. How can God be providing for them? The problem comes down to our understanding of God providing. We like to think that when God provides for an animal, it lives a carefree existence. But would God really be providing what that animal needs? What would it look like if suddenly no animals needed to search for food? The animal kingdom would cease to look like the animal kingdom. God gives animals what they need to be their truest selves, and that is to toil for existence, often unsuccessfully. He knows what they need to be an animal because He made them that way. Likewise, God will not provide for us a carefree existence. He will give us exactly what we need to grow into our truest being, whatever that may look like for each individual. Humans are vastly more complicated than animals and will endure a variety of circumstances, whether poverty, wealth, sickness, health, tension, peace, and everything in between. God will provide exactly what we need as human beings to draw closer to Him.

On a more complicated level, Jesus commands us to forsake the societal systems that have been constructed by the principles of evolution. In Jesus' day there was a rigid class structure instituted by the teachers of the law. After being invited into the house of one of these teachers, Jesus is anointed by a woman far below the teachers in the social hierarchy (Lk 7:36-50). The reaction of the teachers is astonishment, for it is unthinkable to associate with someone so far beneath their inner circle. Using their law, they have created a class system in which they view themselves as superior. In evolution, this could be highly advantageous. Creating a segregated group of people who are passionate about their superiority would provide a significant edge during intertribal conflicts. In this case, it just happened to be the law that was the foundation for this superiority that excluded outsiders. Jesus sharply condemns that type of behavior. He abolishes the entire core of their law, which is based on "cleanliness," by revealing the foolishness in the ideas behind it (Mk 7:1-23). A sense of superiority when viewing one's own community in contrast to everyone else, even though strongly favored by evolution, has no place in the life preached by Jesus.

In many cases Jesus proclaims a life that overcomes the principles of the flesh, but at the same time it is not a complete forsaking of all things physical. One would expect to find that Jesus abandoned all things pertaining to the flesh. Yet, he not only picks wheat for food on the Sabbath (Mk 2:23), but also miraculously feeds thousands of people (Lk 9:16). Something as fundamental to the flesh as food is not abandoned by his ministry. For all the warnings not to be ruled by the flesh, whether through riches, security, worry, or social class, he fully intends for us to remain alive in the flesh. It is not a matter of killing the flesh, in which case starvation would be pursued, but rather having authority over the power of the flesh. We are to give the flesh what it needs, not everything it craves.

Unique from our treatment of the physical world in general, Jesus preaches on our relationships with other people. His entire ministry places a high regard on relationships with other people, as can be seen from his rebuke of anger, lust, and revenge (Mt 5). All of these are factors that can ravage relationships, and, not surprisingly, they find positive selection in evolution. Survival of a community requires traitors to be fiercely banished and repercussions sought after any wrong-doings. Being quick-tempered is certainly a superior survival technique to unconditional forgiveness, and yet Jesus instructs people to forgive relentlessly (Lk 17:4). The power of anger, with its ability to break relationships and improve survival, is to be guarded against.

Servanthood is another pillar of Jesus' ministry. The first will be last and the greatest must become a servant of all (Lk 18:14; Lk 22:26; Mk 9:35). The principles of evolution find universal servanthood ludicrous. Surely there are situations where service to others is in the best interest of an individual's genetic heritage. Most notable is the care provided in family relationships, in which at least pieces of genetic heritage are shared among individuals. There are also situations in which service is beneficial because of reciprocal kindness. But the kind of servanthood Jesus proclaims is disastrous for survival. If a source of food becomes available after a long famine, serving others by allowing them to eat first could result in not getting fed. Sacrificing well-being for the benefit of strangers in a highly strained environment is unknown by evolution and proclaimed by Jesus.

Most central to relationships in the ministry of Jesus is love. On the surface this appears mildly agreeable with evolutionary principles. Individuals can often become invested in the lives of others through mutual kindness, and the euphoric feelings of love are powerful motivators for sex. A preaching that propagates love hardly seems at odds with evolution. But this mistakes the core of the love preached by Jesus. The love he instills demands one's entire devotion to valuing the well-being of an individual to an equal amount in the case of other humans, and to an unimaginably greater amount in the case of God (Mk 12:29-31). At its core, the love preached by Jesus is at odds with evolution. To the flesh, it is unthinkable to value other people to an extent that equals the value given to oneself, for it is impossible for them to contribute to one's genetic heritage an equal amount. Loving as Jesus loves is to defy the principles of the flesh and can only be accomplished with the spirit in rightful authority through God's saving grace.

Indeed, love is the foundation of Jesus' entire preaching (and ministry). To be unconditionally devoted to caring for the well-being of other people causes every other act of restraining the flesh to fall into place. When devoted to people, we are not consumed by riches, or worried about our provisions, or building a social hierarchy, or quick to retribution, or resistant to servanthood. Practicing the love of Jesus is removing the cornerstone of the flesh. It is through treating other people as more than simply another animal that the flesh loses its power. And why does Jesus command that we treat other people as more than animals? Quite simply, because they are far more than just another animal. There is a spirit within humans that is the turning point for love. Without it, Jesus' words would be hollow. It is in recognizing that humans are far more than another animal that we have a foundation for defying the normal principles of the flesh. Perceiving a spirit imparted by God in other people (as well as in ourselves) is an exceedingly vital tool for subduing the power of genetic selfishness simply because the spiritual realm is beyond the reach of evolution. Crucially, without the grace of God any effort is still useless, for no amount of hopeful thoughts can overcome the flesh without Christ's redemption. But being constantly aware of the spirit residing within the physical is decisive in uprooting the flesh and continuing Jesus' ministry.

His Resurrection

After Jesus had been raised from the dead, he appeared to his followers on multiple occasions. Notably, he possessed a body that mirrored his earthly body (Lk 24: 37-43), and this leads to a troubling prospect. Will the handiwork of evolution characterize our existence for all eternity? Our resurrection will mirror that of Jesus, suggesting that our current bodies will resemble those bestowed upon us in the hereafter. If our current bodies are to have a bearing on our existence for the rest of eternity, why wouldn't God have specially made them instead of leaving it up to the process of evolution? To begin, it can be recognized that this question assumes that evolution can operate on its own and that God only uses the final products. But this is misleading. Neither evolution, nor any aspect of the natural world, happens without God's decree. Although it seems that the characteristics of our bodies were shaped by environmental pressures, these were really the secondary agents God used to create His end product.

However, there is a complementary perspective that can be taken in regard to evolution having a lasting impact on eternity. Essentially, our physical bodies are irrelevant. If in the Garden of Eden there was the potential for perfection even though the humans lived in bodies made by the dirty process of evolution, who is to say it will be any different on the new earth? Humanity is defined by the spirit's relation to God; the specific state of the body is irrelevant. Surely, a body is important, because it gives the spirit a vehicle through which to find existence, but its specific state is not central to being considered uniquely human. The body is the medium through which the spirit is able to interact with a physical world that its existence is otherwise not contingent upon. Formation through evolution is irrelevant, for the body is not deemed perfect based on the process that made it, but rather through the state of the spirit in relation to God. Living in evolved bodies in the new earth should hardly be troubling, for our ultimate perfection will be found in spiritual communion with God.

THE DISTINCTION

If humankind is no better than the rest of creation after the fall, why does it not appear that way? Humans chose to become enslaved within an animal flesh, consuming the spirit such that it could have no concept of God. But at the same time, humans, even in a fallen state, appear to be above the rest of creation. What is it exactly that makes humans different from other animals? Essentially, symbolic thought is what sets us apart. It is the foundation for language, art, relationships, and complex systems of thought. It is the ability to have a physical object represent much more than the sum of its parts when considered in the mind. For example, a word is only a collection of lines and curves (or sound pulses), but it is infused with additional significance when seen by a mind that can think symbolically. Since symbolic thought is what sets humans apart, the high position of the human race that has led to unique artifacts such as rising towers or intricate electrical connections is a matter of intellect.

Although it may appear that humans are only separated from other animals by a brain that happens to be more developed, a crucial insight is made by recognizing that symbolic thought is the root of religion. Being able to construct an object or look at an aspect of nature and consider it God is only possible by imparting it with something it does not intrinsically carry. This would seem to imply that symbolic thought and the ability to consider God are one in the same. Yet, this means that symbolic thought is not simply a matter of intellect, for it is clear that an animal should possess no ability to ponder God. So what's the alternative source of human uniqueness? Throughout civilization, God may have been opening the eyes of people through the Holy Spirit, allowing them to contemplate God and at the same time have a spirit that begins to reach beyond its bondage in the flesh. Granted, most people then turn from God to a path of material worship of one form or another, but just the fact that they are able to have a thought of God is enough to think that God must be giving the spirit some minuscule amount of freedom. The ability to think symbolically and the ability to consider God are connected such that we have been reflecting more than simply an animal only because God has slightly lessened the slavery to our bodies.

Consider the progress of the human race. It has been relatively slow until the past few thousand years, especially in the framework of the first humans originating forty to one hundred thousand years ago. Is it only a coincidence that the progress of human civilization has grown exponentially in relatively the same time that God has become more present in people through the Holy Spirit? That's not to say that only those who are following God are able to have achievements of great impact in life. But God's general presence in society, now that everyone beyond the Israelites is able to have a close connection to God, is enough to suppose that His increased presence allowed greater symbolic thought and a more extensive separation from animals.

Current human society seems light-years away from that of other animals, but it has not always been that way. Ancient cultures are distinguished in the fossil records largely by complex tools, which could be made by a very smart animal. So it is not as if a snapshot of them next to the rest of the animal kingdom would be vastly disproportionate, as it is today. There were generations of hominids, like the Neanderthals, who were not significantly behind that progress of the human race. Aboriginal Tasmanians had a culture and technology that were practically equivalent to those of Neanderthals, even though they were entirely human and therefore must have had a spirit. At the same time, there are additional clues of symbolic thought in human cultures, such as shells pieced with holes for jewelry, bones hollowed for a flute, and art on cave walls. But even then, these remnants are both sparse and nothing compared to the objects built by the human mind today. Ancient human populations were not significantly different from other animals, even if small amounts of symbolic art are considered.

When considering two animals, one with a spirit and one without, it is perplexing that they would be so similar. Many people investigating day-age creation (God creating species over millions of years) strive to find evidence that humans in the fossil record were vastly distinct from all other hominids. This is entirely understandable, for humans were shaped into the image of God, so it is natural to expect them to act differently. Unfortunately, many ancient human cultures (some witnessed in modern times) do not show obvious signs of having a spirit beyond sparse remnants, at least not like the discrepancy apparent today. With the perspective of humanity falling into the flesh, it is not surprising in the slightest that humans would behave quite similar to other animals. A human chained in slavery to a body should not act significantly different from its nearest animal relatives, because the spirit has no authority over the body. When the flesh is in complete control, there will be no evidence that a spirit is hidden inside the body. Only when God frees the spirit to have influence over the body is the human able to possess increased amounts of the symbolic thought that reflects the spirit and separates humans from the rest of the animal kingdom.

A crucial distinction needs to be made. There must be a difference, although possibly subtle, between having a concept of God and being able to seek Him as He truly is. The vast majority of humanity has a concept of God, which is beyond the capabilities of an animal, but only the select are opened to see the majesty of His truth. The Jews in Jesus' day had a concept of God, and yet Jesus maintained that they would not come to Him unless the Father drew them. In that sense, the freedom of a human spirit to seek God must be two fold. First we are given the ability to consider God and consequentially exhibit the symbolic thought that is characteristic of humans. Then we are led to a true and personal connection with God through His beckoning. This is often distinguished as general and specific revelation. Inevitably, this begins to question the relationship between God's providence and human free will, but this is no less a problem from an evolutionary framework than it is traditionally. Even when the human spirit is slightly freed from the body by God to exercise symbolic thought and ponder the divine, it must be maintained that we have no capability to truly pursue God without His calling.

SALVATION

Since the time of Jesus, the route to salvation has been clearly spelled out in the Bible. Trusting in Christ for the forgiveness of sins, accompanied by submitting to His lordship, is the only way for someone to be saved and therefore liberate the spirit from bondage to the sinful flesh. However, an evolutionary perspective widens this point of view. For thousands of years humans existed without any mention of Jesus or even righteousness through observing the law. There is a sense in which considering the salvation of those outside God's specific revelation is frivolous, because Jesus has made the path to God clear. Yet, understanding the salvation of humanity in general may not only provide important overarching principles, but is only considerate in light of the amount of people in that category.

If humanity began at least forty thousand years ago (perhaps more), then the number of people who lived either before Abraham or in geographic isolation from Jerusalem must be enormous. Even though the actual population numbers would be vague, what's clear is that the eras of humanity before Jesus vastly outweigh the time span since. Humanity existed, and struggled to exist, long before Jesus came and even long before the covenant with Abraham. So the question becomes one of how salvation was attained for the generations upon generations of humans who never heard the word of God, for they certainly cannot be excluded from salvation simply because of their place in history.

A good place to start is to understand general revelation, in which God opens the eyes of all humanity to be able to perceive His existence. Along with the recognition of deity comes the conviction that we fall significantly short of the deity's standards. Specifically, the flesh we live in produces this apparent distance from God. Everything we succumb to in the flesh creates an underlying, yet subtle, feeling that something is missing. General revelation provokes the thought that there is a gap between us and deity, as rooted in the foreign and incomplete nature of the flesh. In opening our eyes to ponder Him, God is simultaneously causing the first inklings that question the innocence of the flesh. A moral law is born in which the most extreme lusts of the flesh become universally condemned, with additional underlying guilt for the seemingly less destructive desires of the flesh. The caution toward these actions of the flesh are the opposite of what evolution would want, so general revelation essentially creates a whisper that we are aliens in these bodies.

How does this relate to salvation found through general revelation? When confronted with a sense that following the flesh puts us short of a connection with God, most people nonetheless continue to pursue the flesh. So righteousness from the perspective of general revelation must come first through recognizing the flesh of this world for what it is and the distance it creates from God. Everyone surely thinks that certain areas of this world are corrupt. But the difference comes in admitting that no matter how good something might look, if it was built by the flesh alone, then it is necessarily corrupt and distant from God (with respect to human civilization). Salvation for thousands of years of human populations came first and foremost from having a sense that we are aliens in this world and believing that the corrupt actions of our daily lives are dragging us away from God.

Does the flesh really need to be pinpointed, though? Certainly not, for humanity has only recently come to discover the selfish passion raging through every organism. People living in the ancient past would have no basis for believing the complex situation in which we become chained within the flesh while maintaining a goodness of creation. All that really needs to be recognized is the evil within all of humanity that cannot be escaped. How exactly that evil manifests itself is useful information to have, but coming to the humbling conclusion that there is something in us keeping God at a distance is vastly more important. The first step to approaching God, whether in ancient or modern times, is to recognize that we have no basis for making such an approach. We should have long ago been banished without a second thought. Yet, understanding precisely why we are unable to approach God is useful to consider, and the slavery to the flesh will continue to be the starting point.

Recognizing that the bodies of this world are intrinsically corrupt is not the entirety of salvation. It is not enough to merely realize how low we are, but how Holy God is. Believing in the existence of a God that is above and beyond the consuming destruction of this world spurs on a human to believe that the spirit can be lifted above the flesh. If we were only to recognize the corruption pulsing through us, we would fall back into the desires of the flesh at the hopelessness that freedom is impossible. God opens our eyes to ponder Him, and as a result, we can see not only the depths of our corruption but also the heights of His majesty. Once again the human flesh causes trouble, for we often fall for gods that are not beyond the evil of this world. Even once our corruption is recognized, the most prevalent reaction through the course of human history is to believe in a materialistic god that is only marginally above the evil of this world.

Believing in a transcendent God should lead to the notion that He desires to help when considering salvation from general revelation. Simply noticing there is an entity beyond the evil we are stuck in provides no reason to think we can ever be free from this evil. A true belief in God not only entails Holiness beyond this flesh but also His presence in this world and refusal to forsake humankind. Salvation comes from recognizing that a God who can free us from this evil is working through the world, even if it doesn't appear that way. Those saved in ancient times recognized that the world was corrupt and distant from a God who was vastly beyond the evil and who was not a passive bystander.

Although the objection could be raised that salvation in ancient times stemmed directly and necessarily from general revelation, faith was actually vital. Believing in the goodness of a God that is not readily witnessed necessitates faith and cannot be derived directly from the general revelation that this corrupt world is far from a perfect God. How much easier would it be to believe in the sun god, who appears every day, or the god of rain, who frequently opens the sky? It took faith for people in ancient times to look at the gods of their culture and refuse to believe that God can be limited to an object or a controllable, humanlike entity (such as the Greek gods).

The Bible is relatively quiet on the matters of salvation through general revelation. There is one clear instance in which a man is saved based on general revelation alone, and it comes from the interaction between Abraham and Melchizedek in Genesis 15. Melchizedek is introduced as a priest of God Most High, and the reason for this title becomes clear when he bestows a blessing. By blessing Abraham, he was recognizing the work of God through Abraham, as anticipated by someone who held a strong faith in a divinely active God. Further, he not only followed a God who is "creator of heaven and earth," which would have contradicted many cultural gods of the time, but he also recognized God as the Most High. His faith rested in a God that is beyond anything he could comprehend, not a petty figure under the influence of humankind. And yet, even though this God is higher than the highest height, Melchizedek still maintains faith that He has not forsaken creation, for He was at work through Abraham's victory in battle.

Melchizedek was clearly a man of great faith in God. Abraham recognized this and paid him tribute. The writer of Hebrews drew upon this by illustrating that Christ will be a High Priest like Melchizedek. It is not difficult to say that Melchizedek would have worshiped at the feet of Jesus if given the chance. But it would be foolish to assume that salvation through general revelation must exhibit a faith to the magnitude of that displayed by Melchizedek. To have his priesthood compared with that of Jesus, he must have been reaching to the limits of the faith that can be sustained from general revelation. Surely, it does not take his level of faith to be saved using general revelation alone.

It seems strange to the modern Christian mind that someone could attain salvation outside Jesus and even outside the old covenant. But this should never be troubling. Those saved in ancient times may have had no idea about God's movements in humanity through Abraham/Israel and certainly had no idea how a messiah would save them. Not even the Israelites were able to correctly interpret God's direct word about the messiah. These isolated people may not even have expected a messiah, but this should not be troubling. If individuals hold the previously described beliefs about this world and God's place above it, then they would certainly have welcomed Jesus. This idea is crucial. If a person's place in history doesn't matter, then that person could theoretically be placed in the time of Jesus and accept Him as the one sent by God to offer freedom from the penalty for distrusting Him. The exact placement of this cutoff for salvation among people who never heard of Jesus is only discernable by God. He is the only one who knows how many of the attributes of salvation are required for a person to have followed Christ if given the chance. Surely, each case is different because of the respective cultures each person is brought up in. But we know that God judges each according to what he or she is given, so He is fair and just in examining those who had faith in Him through general revelation.

What does the consideration of general revelation mean for those who are saved through Christ? It appears to simply be a pointless secondary aspect of salvation now that we have Jesus, but it brings up two important ideas. First, it illustrates the foundation of our faith. The progression from seeing the world as corrupt, to believing in a God above it all, to having faith that He is actively moving to bring humans back to Him, leads straight into Abraham and the covenant with man. Oftentimes, we don't understand the steps that led up to the story of redemption in the Bible and why the sequence is so important. If we understood the principles that have been the path to salvation for ancient people, we would appreciate the story of the Bible much more. It takes recognizing the corruption of this world and yearning for a transcendent God to make Himself known to fall face-down before Jesus. Second, the amount of time when general revelation was the only way to salvation should make us thankful to live in the time of Christ. It would have been much more difficult for ancient people to have faith in a God they couldn't see, and therefore attain salvation, than it is for us to witness Christ and have faith in a God standing before us. The time after Christ is truly a privileged time in which to live.

THE LAW

After slavery in Egypt, God gave the law to the Israelite nation for two main reasons. In order to be God's chosen people, they needed a means to distinguish themselves for all other nations so as to not be absorbed into the rest of the world and lose their unique purpose. The series of rigid instructions for daily living and temple practices was intended to set aside a people for the one true God among an environment of fluid kingdoms. But the law was also intended to reshape the character of God's people. By displaying the distinct perfection of God through a collection of commands, people were meant to become humble and entirely dependent upon God. When God unveils His perfection and it becomes clear that we are vastly incapable of attaining it by human means, we should fall prostrate before God to save us from ruin. The law was a beautiful device not only for national politics, but also for drawing people closer to God by revealing His character and allowing them to recognize the meekness of humankind.

But we know this is not what happened with the human response to the law. To be sure, this was by no fault of God. He provided a very real way to draw closer to Him and grow into people of righteousness. We were the ones who took a good thing and corrupted it. With the law in hand, our transgressions only increased. What was intended to bring life only brought death, for when presented with the right course of action, we become inundated with an inclination to do the opposite (Rm 7:7-25). There is a simple explanation for this. We are like children filled with a corrupt mind-set to rebel against our parents. When told we are unable to sit in a chair, there is nothing we want to do more than sit in the chair. We are unable to follow the commandments of God because our sinful nature manufactures a desire to do the opposite of God's will. But is this the entirety of the explanation for our misuse of the law? Evolution would suggest it isn't. The law interacted with our evolutionary heritage in a unique manner that inclined humans to respond to the law in a harmful fashion. How did this happen? And more importantly, why was the story of God's redemptive plan staged in such a manner?

The Ten Commandments (Ex 20:1-17) are a useful example of how evolution influences the law. Seven of the commandments—idolatry (twice), murder, adultery, theft, false testimony, and covetousness—have strong evolutionary connections. There are reasons evolution would support all of these actions due to genetic advantage, as already discussed. Some of the reasons are more apparent than others, but commands against these all find significant conflict with the principles of evolution. If we are slaves to the flesh, as previously established, it would be expected that living according to these restrictions can be difficult. This is how the law was received by the Israelites, as can be seen by the religious leaders of Jesus' day having difficulty with commands such as these. The remaining three commandments (not misusing the LORD's name, keeping the Sabbath, and honoring father and mother) are lacking in evolutionary connections. There is no reason within the constructs of genetic selfishness to be averse to keeping one day Holy, or refraining from certain words, or honoring father and mother. Commands such as these were not particularly difficult for the Israelites to obey.

What general idea does this segregation in the Ten Commandments convey? There are two types of commands in the law: those that contradict evolution and those that have no bearing on evolution. Those that run contrary to evolution are the ones modern Christianity is familiar with because they are the focal points of our daily sin, as already discussed. But there is another realm of laws not adopted by modern Christians that was central to the Israelite nation. Aspects of life such as temple practices, Sabbath regulations, and matters of personal cleanliness were all very significant, as displayed by the religious leaders in Jesus' day. These laws lack a bearing on evolution, for they have no effect on genetic heritage. Unsurprisingly, this second category of laws was adopted passionately by the people and, in general, followed rigorously. They were slaves to the flesh, just as we are today, not to these unaffected factors. So obeying this second set of laws was relatively easy because the chains of their slavery were not specifically restricting them in these areas. Yet, the question remains: What does this dichotomy between relatively easy laws and those that battle the flesh have to do with the misuse of the law?

Think of it like training a puppy, where the puppy is humanity and the trainer is God. There are things the puppy really wants to do, like bark, jump up on people, relieve itself in the house, bite people, and run around like crazy. The trainer sets out to correct these behaviors by rebuking them. So now the puppy may still do these forbidden things because instincts are hard to break, but the trainer is able to gradually reduce them. Suppose the trainer begins working on a number of other "tricks," like getting the puppy to sit or lie down. There is nothing within the instincts of the puppy that resist such actions, so it is able to obey dutifully, and positive feedback is applied through the pleasure of the trainer. At this point nothing may radically change because a puppy is relatively simple. But suppose the puppy is complex, like humans, and is given not one or two additional tricks, but a whole slew of rules that are easy to follow. The puppy begins to think that its abilities might be useful after all. A significant amount of positive feedback from the trainer for commands that are easy to follow makes the puppy confident that its actions are good in the eyes of the trainer. Naturally, it returns to breaking those commands that contradict its instinct. Imagine the thoughts of the puppy: "If so many things I can do are good, why wouldn't those things I want to do be good as well?"

Humans were given a law that both rebukes their natural instincts and reinforces the idea that their abilities are good. If human hands are able to follow a significant amount of guidelines for life that are pleasing to God, maybe the other constructs of human hands are good as well. A confidence in our flesh is thus produced, which leads to increased submission to the principles of the flesh God commands us to overcome. As we begin to think we are naturally good due to apparently good abilities, we express our natural character because it must similarly be good. Yet, we are sorely mistaken. Our natural inclinations in the flesh are not good. By partaking in the desires of the flesh because it seems justified, we are constructing a barrier between us and God. The law, taken in conjunction with evolution, produces a confidence in the flesh that indulges the principles of the flesh and creates distance between us and God, because the supremacy of the flesh is what separates us from God in the first place.

Why would God have induced such a scenario? As stated, God is not to blame for the misuse of the law. He gave the Israelites a legitimate way to draw closer to Him. Yet, He must have known what was going to happen. He gave Pharaoh the opportunity to set the Israelites free, even though it was destined for His power to be displayed through the plagues of Egypt. God has a plan for everything, even our missteps. So why was it similarly destined for the Israelites to misuse the law? God knew what He was doing in giving them a law that could prey upon evolutionary instincts, for the law was never the final solution. He knew all along that His Son would need to be sacrificed as the atonement of all humanity, and for that to happen there needed to be a people who would crucify him. There needed to be a society of people so hardened toward the way of God that when His Son came to proclaim the Kingdom of God, there would be revolt. The law, through its misuse by the Israelites, was able to accomplish this objective. Surely, the Israelites are not the only society that would have crucified Jesus, but many of them probably wouldn't. God was creating a people that would without a doubt crucify His Son so that salvation could be for all humanity. By becoming absorbed with the flesh, the Israelites were hostile towards Jesus' message of freedom from the principles of the flesh and fulfilled the role of necessary hostility. They thought they were superior to all humanity, when in reality they were carrying the burden for the rest of humanity.

NATURE

Physical existence is evil. That is what the Christian evolutionary framework outlined thus far would seem to conclude. The dominion of our physical bodies and the selfishness those bodies operate under is what separates us from God, so the natural world built by evolution must be evil. Without these dreaded bodies dragging us down, we would be fit to stand in the presence of God. And not only are the spiritual implications of bodies wired by natural selection evil, but natural selection itself is very easily seen as an evil force among nature. It has been common among Christians to suppose the predator and prey relationship of nature resulted after evil was introduced at the fall not because it is supported by the narrative, but because it seems to neatly stow away the elephant in the room: How can God's creation be good when it is so cruel? This world's nature is a terrible place for us, with dangers lurking even in microbes invisible to the eye and slavery awaiting us in flesh built by the selfishness of natural selection. The antidote is clear: to be swept away from this self-destructive world to the spiritual realm just beyond the sky, where there is a euphoria awaiting those in the presence of God. But if we are to escape to this euphoria beyond the sky, we're going to have to do it without God's help, for He made us with our feet fully planted in the ground, a ground that is evil only in the misguided constructs of our minds.

Cruelty, or at least the appearance of cruelty, in nature is widespread among humanity's perceptions. Few can watch a mother kill off the weakest of her children so the others have a better chance of survival and not feel a

SMITH

nagging sense that something is wrong. Nature shouldn't be this way. The runt of the litter shouldn't be destined to death; the alpha male shouldn't inflict doom on subordinates; parasites shouldn't devour animals from the inside out. Many people would say they have no problem with death in nature to a large degree; it's only the highly disturbing acts that are framed as cruel and unjust. But this misses the point, because it is not a question of the scale of cruelty in nature. It was all shaped by the same underlying principle of genetic propagation, and having a problem with any of it means having a problem with all of it. Natural selection may try to give an appearance that is innocent, but when we see its true colors, we are disgusted. Nature from the perspective of evolution seems like a very uncoordinated blacksmith fumbling around in his shop. For every soot-covered tool that's made, two or three are knocked to the ground or destroyed.

What we'd really like is for the messiness of nature to be cleaned up. In fact, we've done just that in the creation of zoos. Why can't all creatures just leave one another alone and live their own happy existence? This straight forward and clean nature would fit so much better with the constructs of the human mind. But that is exactly the problem. Nature does not answer to the overarching principles of our minds. It is the product of a mind far beyond what our minds could ever encompass. Nature is not deemed good based on our standards; it answers only to God. Having a problem with a creation that appears to lack goodness ignores the fact that we have superimposed our own definition of good, which may not be that of God. Does God look upon a runt struggling for survival with disgust? In all likelihood, He does not. Countless creatures have struggled for survival since the beginning of life, and if there was a standard here that was not up to God's codes, He would not have decreed it good. There is a beauty in nature that is beyond what the constructs of our minds can grab onto, and it redefines the goodness of the natural around what God sees, not what small parts we are able to grasp. Yes, humans can at times find deep appreciation in the beauty of nature, but in the end we lock onto the isolated "evil" acts just as when we look at human society. But there is not something wrong in nature like there is something wrong in human society. God looks upon nature and sees the beauty He has been constructing since the beginning, which is obviously less than can be said of human society.

If creation is not evil because it was created by God, how are we to relate to it? As difficult as it is to accept the beauty in the harshness of natural selection, considering the implications of this only adds weight to the difficulty. Are we justified in simply jumping on board with this abuse? Every other organism is in the business of abusing its surroundings for the propagation of its personal genes, only seeking partnership when it is of benefit. Why can't we do the same? The rampant consumption of nature seems like a reasonable conclusion. But this ignores the fact that God made us to be more than just another animal in the progression of evolution. Having a spirit means being on another level from the rest of nature where there is the responsibility of an overseer, not a tyrant. God lifted us above nature so that we could willfully glorify Him and be His representatives among creation. To revert back to abuse is to glorify our physical existence over the calling given to us from God. It is a side effect of living like every other animal because we decided to put our flesh above God. Jumping on board with the harshness of natural selection is only a possibility because of the distance we have fallen from God in this flesh and should not be considered a reasonable option.

How, then, are we to relate to nature? Although abuse is not an option, some utilization is still necessary. Having a body means having physical needs that cannot be ignored, and living in a creation beautiful to God does not negate His love for human beings above the rest of creation. Our needs are rightfully given priority because God has made it clear that we are a priority. Utilization of nature is necessary for our existence to continue, but in light of the beauty in creation upheld by God, we should at the very least preserve the original order to whatever degree possible. We need to take from creation, but we don't need to destroy the complex ecosystems that have been evolving together since the beginning. That would be to destroy a beauty ordained by God that was never ours to deface.

Affirming the beauty of nature that can appear cruel is one thing. Maintaining this beauty when it becomes known that the underlying principle throughout nature is the force separating us from God is another entirely. If we are to believe that giving authority to the flesh is what separated us from God, how are we to maintain that the creation that built this flesh is still good? Shouldn't the fact that we are enslaved by something necessitate a passion for destroying it? This inevitably leads to a consideration of the circumstances when the slavery started. If slavery is sparked by the will of the powerful to oppress the weak, it is justifiable for the weak to seek destruction of the powerful. But what if it was flipped? If the weak wished to oppress the powerful, obviously nothing would happen. That is, unless the powerful chose to become enslaved by the weak. In such a case, the powerful would not have anyone to blame but themselves and whatever may have led them to succumbing to the weak. This is just the situation of humanity. The flesh had no authority over us until we gave it that authority. To say the workings of the flesh are evil because they have us in slavery is to skip the step in the story where the real evil occurred: Humanity gave glory to the flesh.

A NEW APPROACH

Where does all this reasoning about the impact of evolution on Christianity lead us? At the outset, it was intended to reconcile evolution with the principles of Christianity. Yet, this was not as simple as imagined. Ironing out the difficulties with animal death before the fall and a human body that lacks unique divinity was not enough. A full understanding of evolution required more. Starting with a recognition of genetic selfishness, a new scenario for the fall of humankind was put forth, resulting in a greater understanding of slavery to sin. The flesh has a much larger role in humanity than simply being a vehicle for our existence. Its supremacy is our source of chains, separating us from almighty God. It is the slavery we fell into, and liberation is the offering of Christ. The lumps on the playing field of evolutionary Christianity have been more than ironed out; a new playing field has been recognized. It is not entirely distinct, for the core principles are the same as always for Christianity. But a greater clarity of the events on the field has been exposed. This supplementary knowledge is both inconsequential and of pivotal utility.

First, let's consider how it is inconsequential. Imagine driving a car that continuously breaks down. It's still drivable, but most of the time it seems to crawl along, sometimes quitting entirely for periods of time. The typical response is to ignore any problems that may arise, for it seems as though the car will always make whatever small comeback is necessary to be barely functional again. All is well, and no meddling is required. But what if the car is to be truly fixed? Obviously, it first needs to be recognized that a mechanic is needed. This is the vastly most important step. Understanding whether it is the engine or the body of the car causing problems is irrelevant without the mechanic, because in this scenario we are incompetent to fix it. Requesting and submitting to a mechanic will lead to the necessary changes without knowledge of the exact details. Acknowledging that there is something terribly wrong with us that creates a separation from God only crossable by Him is vital to human life. It is the foundation for Christ's redemption and has always been the core of Christianity.

What if the mechanic is to be assisted, though? This is where knowledge of the human situation comes to alter our mind-set significantly. Understanding the effects of our evolutionary heritage is hardly irrelevant. In attempting to assist the mechanic, we must have a greater awareness of what is wrong with the car. Surely, humanity has always understood the problems within us to some extent. We can be self-absorbed, quick to anger, power-hungry, and emotionally inconsiderate, along with many other harmful characteristics. But evolution provides a much more enlightening viewpoint. It explains the reason for why these characteristics are so prevalent and inescapable to our existence. It puts a subject to our source of slavery, and in doing so, it provides a deeper understanding of why human life is constantly going off the tracks. It is as if we have always known that the car runs out of fuel too quickly, but now we realize the reason is that the valves have a tendency to leak, or something of that sort. We can now be useful in helping the mechanic breathe new life into a decrepit car, because the grasp we have on human corruption is substantially increased.

With a greater understanding of the sources of struggle in our personal lives comes an enhanced perspective on all humanity. The Christian viewpoint has long maintained that people are separated from God because of their own choices. Compassion necessarily results from observing such a terrible situation and desiring to help. An evolutionary perspective only magnifies this compassion. It is still maintained that people are willfully rejecting the calling of God, but it is not due to an uninfluenced rush in the opposite direction. The human spirit is not merely rejecting God out of pride; it is choosing to glorify something specific above God. We are running to the flesh, not just running away from God or running towards our innermost beings. Our journey from God is through submitting to the torrent of self-serving desires inherent to evolution in nature, which have the remarkable impression of being essential to our existence. We are like children relentlessly holding our special blanket for comfort, unaware that it is killing us. We did not choose this death in a courageous stand of independence, but because we cling with ultimate priority to an object of security that appears entirely innocent. People everywhere are separated from God by something that is dear to them. Bestowing authority on our bodies instead of on God is slowing killing us while we live in the blissful pleasure of a highly developed animal. How can we not be moved to compassion as people search for comfort and pleasure in the flesh like children with a blanket, unaware that it is the vehicle for their separation from almighty God?

Looking at Christianity from the starting point of evolution is not simple. It radically shifts how we understand the sinful nature in humans, while keeping the foundational truths of the Bible firmly intact. Christ is the redeemer who came to bring us into the presence of God after we committed idolatry against Him, and we are utterly helpless without Him. And yet, if evolution is to be true, it could provide a significant breakthrough. If we were created through genetic selfishness like every other animal, scientific study of the natural world has brought us to a discovery that has been unknown for millennia. After Adam and Eve glorified the flesh, they likely had an understanding of the power pulsing in nature because it had just become the source of their slavery. But even then, they likely did not possess a concept of evolution (who knows how they perceived nature?). Thus, we could be uncovering a truth that has eluded humanity from the beginning. Thousands of years and countless generations passed before our intellects could unearth the truth about nature's evolution. It is a discovery that could reshape the viewpoint of Christianity. We have the potential to understand the wretched state of humanity better than ever before.

ABOUT THE AUTHOR

My upbringing, like that of many others born into a Christian environment, landed on creationism by default. When it became clear that I was scientifically minded, it was only natural for me to use my abilities to combat rampant "evolutionism." But the observations of nature just didn't add up. Now an engineer, I solve problems. And evolution is a glaring problem for Christianity in ways people don't even realize. I do what I can to wrestle with these problems, not because I am qualified, but because no one else will.

www.ingramcontent.com/pod-product-compliance
Lightning Source LLC
Chambersburg PA
CBHW071905020426
42331CB00010B/2686